Operations Team Leadership

For a complete list of Management Books 2000 titles,
visit our web-site on http://www.mb2000.com

Operations Team Leadership

Graham R Little PhD AFNZIM

2000

First published in 2000 by Management Books 2000 Ltd
Cowcombe House
Cowcombe Hill
Chalford
Gloucestershire GL6 8HP
Tel. 01285 760 722
Fax. 01285 760 708
E-mail: mb2000@compuserve.com

Printed and bound in Great Britain by Biddles, Guildford

British Library Cataloguing in Publication Data is available

ISBN 1-85252-336-0

Contents

7

Offer leadership 131

Preface

Welcome. You are one of the exceptional people of the world who actually read the preface. In reading this book and acting on the ideas in it, you will be taking steps to fulfilling your potential as a manager and fulfilling some of the goals and aims that have shaped what I have done for thirty years. I gain much fulfilment and quiet satisfaction from seeing and knowing that people have gained, grown and developed from things I have done with them and said to them.

This book is one of a series, with several yet to come. I have for many years been primarily involved in doing a lot for a few, through personal and direct involvement with people. This series is a concerted effort to bring my thought to a wider, indirect audience. I think that several points of philosophy make my thought different. I dislike fads, always have. So I have sought timelessness in the works – things a manager should be doing now, and still be doing in years to come. So this series is not intended to be the 'latest fad', nor the flavour of the month in management thinking. Business is a long-term, highly repetitious activity, frequently requiring people to do the same thing today, tomorrow and the next day and next. So I try to ensure my work is based on the 'reality bites', the simple, disciplined things that have to be done and done again. I also believe that management is often made overly complicated in a conceptual sense. In my experience, the really hard part is living out the things that, as a manager, one knows should be lived out, rather akin to Daniel Goldberg's emotional intelligence. If in addition to the demands on the will, the spirit and self-discipline, the concept is also complicated, then the request on the manager is becoming nigh impossible. So I have sought simple concepts, focusing emphasis on living them out.

The books are based on my personal experience. Most of this has been good, but I have also lost a company and lost a lot of money, which was not good. I learned, and this has added another dimension to my thinking and my work. I did not know it at the time, but looking back, I lived as I did as a process of gaining experience. Frequently I could have chosen safer paths and secure options. I did not, and if I had, then I could never have written this work in this way. Like a good novelist who researches the people and their place, so I did my research, real time.

The first few books, five in all, consist of one completely new concept, *The Five Steps to Better Business Leadership* and four books based on earlier works. These latter four have been updated and strengthened from my experience and development of my thinking since they were first written. They have a harder 'edge'. Three of the books *Sales Team Leadership, Operations Team Leadership* and *Retail Team Leadership* have the same introduction. This is done for the reason that the great majority of managers will buy only one of these – they are either in sales, operations or retail, and unlikely to be in two at any one time.

So what should a manager read of this series? A full development program would cover the books *The Five Steps of Business Leadership Success, Management Team Leadership* and one of *Sales, Operations* or *Retail Leadership*. They all offer different things each from a different point of view. Three books is a lot in one sitting, so reading them and working through them could take quite some time. It is important that not only do you read, but also think about how to act on what you read and where and how the ideas can be applied in your business and team. If you want a better result, then you need to act differently from how you acted yesterday. These books will guide you on what to do and how to do it. They can help with more will, but mostly they describe how to achieve greater skill.

Forthcoming books concern motivation, training, leadership and the will to win. The first two directly continue the work begun in the first five books. The other two are more general, somewhat focused on more personal development issues – issues, can I say, that are more spiritual (in a totally non-religious sense). This goes to the heart of my experience of good leaders – almost inevitably they were hard on the outside, committed to the success of their enterprise, doing what had to be done. But these leaders were soft on the inside, their humanity and sensitivity evident under their self-discipline, and offering something beyond today's pound. They were people to whom one could and did relate, but they also filled others with confidence that the enterprise would thrive under their leadership and that you as a person would always be given careful thought if ever there were problems needing hard decisions.

So I entrust you to my work, and hope for you the very best you are able to be.

Graham Little, Auckland, NZ, April 2000

12

Introduction

Getting a better result

This book series focuses on the thinking and behaviour of the management team and key staff. It improves operating profit by altering the focus, and the actions of these staff are changed in the direction of improved operating profit.

There are four books in the series, **Management Team Leadership**, **Sales Team leadership**, **Operations Team Leadership** and **Retail Store Leadership**. A fifth book, **The Five Steps To Business Leadership Success** provides the overview for all of the four 'leadership' books and offers an analysis of a simple yet extremely practical theory of management and organisation that leads to simple yet effective guidelines on how to act as a business leader to get the best possible results from a team.

If you believe there is potential to improve the performance of yourself your team and your business, then this book series will assist you to achieve that result.

Business Momentum

Think of a business as a flywheel – once going, it is not hard to keep it going in the same direction at the same speed. But it is very hard to increase speed or change direction. The momentum of a business lies in the behaviour and thinking of the staff and in the behaviour and thinking of the customers and potential customers.

Maintaining the momentum of a business is not difficult. To increase that momentum requires the injection of focused effort. This energy that is needed to increase the momentum can and must come from the management team and key staff. This 'extra effort', that is the effort to increase the momentum of a business, I call the '***creative*** *input'* by the team. I define creativity in business as that effort that increases the momentum of a business to greater, permanent increases in operating profit or market share or return on funds employed, or whatever factor is selected by the senior management.

What this book can do for you

If you picked up this book, then obviously you were looking for something. Somewhere, conscious or not, there is a quest within you. Perhaps it is to better yourself, perhaps to get a better result from your team or business, or perhaps, like I have been at times in my life, you are looking for something without knowing you are looking and without knowing what it is you are looking for.

Let me tell you something about this book series. It can do four things for someone willing to think about what it has to say and who has at least a little of the questing in them.

✓ The books can strengthen the attitude of striving and self-belief on which all success must ultimately rest. They can and will move you forward toward the best possible for you. Thus the books can facilitate emotional skills.

✓ Importantly, the books explore many important concepts and conceptual structures. We are predominantly a thinking species. The more effectively we think about situations, the more effective we are likely to act toward that situation. The books can and will develop conceptual skills.

✓ An important philosophy developed throughout the books is that business is only rational in retrospect. Fundamentally, the forward momentum of a business is emotional, and the crucial forward direction, often day by day, is created. By exploring how to improve insight and identify opportunity, the books develop creative skills.

✓ Finally, much of the books are devoted to implementing the ideas and opportunities that emerge. Repeatedly I find that the best businesses are those with every day creative talent who can and do implement with care and precision the ideas before them. Often those ideas are simple, even basic. Seldom are the ideas very clever. The books will develop your skills at making real the sharp effective ideas that can increase the operating profit in your business.

How to best use the books

There are three necessary factors needed for effective action: knowing what to do, knowing how to do it and having the will to get it done. Having picked up the book, there is some sense of quest in you that is all that is needed to begin. It is a myth that we must be motivated and inspired to achieve. Think of mowing the lawns or doing some other chore that you do not think is rewarding but must be done. Often I find with such chores that once I get started I find it is not so bad, and at the end I look back and think, 'well that's a good job done, it wasn't bad, I almost enjoyed it'. What it took to get me going was the disciplined kick-start. Once I got going, I became more motivated. I think this is general – motivation follows action, not the other way around.

The introduction provides the guide to what to do to improve the bottom line of your business. It is based on the idea of profit profile developed by John Tracy in his book *Profit Dynamics* (Ref 17). It is a simple yet very effective tool for assessing the key factors that influence operating profit and for exploring how to manipulate those factors to increase operating profit. Having established what, the books then consider how and build the will to keep at it.

Goal focused

The technique is very goal-focused because the process I adopt is based on the proposition that for every goal there are behaviours that must be acted out if the goal is to be achieved. And this applies to all goals, whether in sports, business, and life generally. I call this the **goal⬅➡action** principle and also the **fundamental principle of organisation** (see *The Five Steps to Successful Business Leadership*).

The development of professional conduct is thus to make the goals clear, then to identify the behaviours most likely to facilitate the goals,

15

and finally, to review with the people whether or not they are acting out the behaviours with the level of commitment needed to achieve the result. For example, if you wanted to be an internationally competitive swimmer, then you need to spend a great deal of time in a swimming pool with due commitment. Going through the motions simply won't cut it, in sport or business.

Personal development and the importance of challenge

Too often training and development is conducted in a passive environment where the urgency to change is low. Consider for a moment when a person loses a close family member. It is quite typical for that person afterwards to say how they feel they have grown, and how they are now able to cope with more than they could before the tragic loss. The growth is a result of the struggle to cope, to get through the days doing what must be done, and the discipline to manage one's emotions and urges, not to give in.

The same principle applies to developing greater leadership and refining the professional conduct in a business. It is refining the focus on 'doing what must be done', rather than 'doing what I feel like' or 'doing just enough'. I can guarantee one thing, that if you invest in these ideas, if you take a non-passive approach to your own development as a leader, if you challenge yourself, then the investment will be repaid. You are worthy of investing in yourself, but you must challenge yourself in terms of your thinking and the disciplined nature of your actions.

Offering a challenge to business teams

The principle of a challenge to facilitate growth is applied to business teams through a process of presenting to the team a *'creative statement'*. This is a statement from the team leader requesting greater performance from the team and specifying the level of improvement he or she expects.

Thus the starting point for facilitating improved management in your business is the question: *is there any aspect of business performance that you would like to see improved and by how much?*

This becomes the creative challenge for the team. We need to do the same with ourselves, that is to challenge our own performance, raise our own expectations of ourselves, not to the point of being impossible but to the point where it stretches us. In the striving to achieve, we grow as people and as business leaders.

Improvements at the edge

Most businesses are well run. If there were something obvious to do that would improve performance, it would have been done. Also, I find that in most businesses, the people do things 80% effectively 80% of the time. But what would benefit the business is to have them doing things 90% effective 90% of the time. This I call improvement at the edge. The effort required is exponential, that is going from 80:80 to 90:90 is as hard as getting to 80:80 in the first place.

Perhaps, above all else it is this philosophy of striving, the clear cut attitude exhibited in behaviour that we can always do better that makes the crucial difference between the average team and the great team. It follows that the ability to instil this attitude into a team is what makes the difference between the average leader and the great leader.

Team Leader as coach

For the book series to succeed for you, you must commit yourself to improved performance. Once you are committed, and if you are a team leader, then you ask your team for greater performance. If asked, people will generally feel that they are working hard now and that there is little or no room for improvement. It is stressed that team leaders must decide the level of performance they wish to achieve in their team. It is the same process as a coach working with an athlete. If the judgement is that the athlete is better than he or she is achieving, then the coach must place that athlete under the appropriate, balanced pressure. The coach sets the standard and draws acceptance from the athlete that if the right things are done at the right time, then the standard will be realised. This is a highly emotionally circumstance, triggered by the creative statement. The coach must be firm in the face of 'but we are working hard already'.

At that point, business is not a democracy. It is the great

leader/coach who draws people beyond their comfort zones and guides their achievement to levels they did not think were possible. They feel good, the coach feels good and the results are good. But these strong, satisfied feelings are after the event. The leader/coach must be firm, with insight, understanding and the strength of patience, and must show the way through the tensions and uncertainties that inevitably result when a team sets high targets for itself.

Bridging the gap between knowing how to do it and doing it

The process to use is one of people applying the skills and understanding they have. Seldom are people making the most of that which they already know and understand. Frequently I hear managers say 'but they have been trained'. Seek to bridge this gap between what people know and what they do. Focus can be one of improving performance, rather than on 'training them' – reshaping their behaviour on the job with the tools they have, rather than training them in the tools in the first place.

Training and development using own job as a case study

The process is a blend of facilitation and consulting. The team is undergoing training in the sense that general principles are reviewed and discussed. The vehicle for facilitating the discussion is a case study that happens to be their own team and the jobs of the people in the workshop. This process is very effective, bringing to the fore the practical, real-world issues of accountability, politics, focus and urgency so difficult to reproduce in a typical training environment.

Beginning with the Management Team

I repeatedly find that an effective place to start is with the Management Team and key staff. This is the key team of any business. Whether it consists of two people or twenty, the focus, urgency and drive of this team will profoundly effect the performance of the business. Some of the questions to be confronted include the following.

18

- Is it possible to target more operating profit?
- Are we stretching ourselves in the manner we expect of our people?
- As a leadership team of the business, can we be more effective?
- Can we be more creative?

The output is a plan showing how the operating profit is to be improved in the coming twelve months. The amount of the improvement is decided on by the team leader – this I call the '*creative statement*'. Typical would be 'increase operating profit next financial year by £250,000 over and above current budgets and over and above current expectations'. There are two rules: (1) there is to be no capital expenditure; (2) the result is to be achieved by a balanced approach to revenue, direct costs and margin, and overheads. Effectively, the process begins with the profit profile of the business and the creative statement then focuses the team on how the profit profile can be improved. I find that when a team are asked, and expected to stretch their creativity and experience, that the opportunities are uncovered and the learning is significant with a resulting permanent change in the climate or culture of the team.

Sales team	Begins each day with an empty piece of paper and has an excellent day when they fill the paper with orders.
Operations team	Begins each day with a full piece of paper and has an excellent day when they get everything done.
Retail store team	Begins each day with the paper half full and has an excellent day when all the store and administrative work is done and they have given excellent customer service and filled the empty half of the paper with orders.
Management team	Has to make sure that each of the above teams that it is leading has as many excellent days as possible – and to make doubly sure that no team fails to have an excellent day due to anything the management team could have or should have done.

Goals

Below are the typical goals that would be set for a team seeking to stretch its performance.

Creative statement

To increase operating profit by £100,000 over and above current expectations and current budget in the current financial year and for that to build into £250,000 increase in operating profit in the coming financial year.

Goals

☑ To use the demand for improved operating profit to focus, stretch and consolidate team performance.

☑ To review and consolidate team roles and accountabilities.

☑ To review the business processes arising for those roles and to redevelop as deemed appropriate.

☑ To improve each individual person's actioning of his or her role in the team.

☑ Consolidate team actions in relation to the agreed plans and strategy.

Begin by challenging yourself, then draw others in your team to challenge themselves. It is not a passive process, and at times you will hesitate in the face of the turmoil due to uncertainty. At these moments, only faith in oneself and belief in the importance of investing in oneself will provide the needed strength. But if you quietly, gently, firmly just do it, you will be rewarded with greater leadership prowess, better business results and deeper satisfaction with yourself.

Where to Start?

The Need for Focus

It is crucial for key team members to have an accepted and shared conceptual formula that focuses attention on the crucial factors that determine operating profit. The team also needs to develop insight into the interrelationship of those factors and how to manage them to optimise and increase operating profit.

Make It Happen

The difference between administering a business and managing a business is that the administrator merely maintains the status quo. In the modern business environment, that is not enough: the business needs management committed to making things happen to ensure that the business maintains its customers, profits and return on capital.

Accountability

The aim of the management team is to generate sales revenue and turn it into operating profit. Within this, each team member has more particular accountabilities. Specifically, each team member must understand which lines and which parts of lines they are accountable for within the agreed profit profile of the business. It is then the responsibility of that manager to develop the insight, skills and control to manipulate those factors and so allow all members to fulfil their roles within the team's overall aim.

Where team members have a general supporting role – an old-fashioned staff function such as the accountant or HR manager – then the role is defined in those terms, for instance, providing historical data and data projecting the impact of management decisions.

Developing the Team Climate

Managers expect operations or a sales or customer service team to be focused on those factors that ensure that the team achieves its aim. Usually, the people are expected to participate, to stay on the topic, to not let personalities or politics get in the way of improving performance, to monitor performance closely – and to get on and do this with a minimum of supervision, with the team members providing peer pressure on performance. Often, however, the functioning of the management team itself does not follow these ethics.

Then where to start? Start with the management team going back to the basics of determining its aim (to turn revenue into operating profit) and the role of each team member within that aim; to establish a clear profit formula; and for all managers to focus vigorously on managing their portfolios and maximising their contribution to the team's aim. Once these ethics become habit and the success is enjoyed and felt through the business, ask all teams to follow this lead.

> The aim of the management team is to generate sales revenue and turn it into operating profit

Some Crucial Questions

- Do you know the few but essential factors that determine profit and performance?
- Can you pinpoint precisely which changes have the best and worst impact on operating profit?
- Are you absolutely clear on what you need to do to maintain and improve profits?
- Are you absolutely clear what your people must do to improve profits?
- Are your people absolutely clear on what they must do?

Plenty of Activity, but Getting it Right is not Easy (Ref 6)

The following comments are from a US survey of major companies

- Over 50% of senior executives surveyed reported five or more change initiatives in the past 18 months.

- Over 50% reported employee attitudes, buy-ins or resistance to change as the concerns most likely to keep them awake at night.

- 67% of executives reported the initiatives had showed up on the bottom line.

- The employees saw it differently – 75% said their skills had not improved, 49% perceived a drop in morale, and while they generally agreed that profitability had improved, they saw the success of the initiatives as 20% less than their executive counterparts.

- Despite the above, less than 25% of the executives planned initiatives involving employee participation, leadership development, team development or performance systems development. There seems to be two attitudes:

  - making the business profitable in spite of the people, or
  - making the business profitable through the people.

Evidence is accumulating that operating profit is stronger and more consistent when the people are actively supportive of the company and management. (Ref. 1, 2, 3, 4, 5, 6, 7, 8, 9, 10, 11, 12, 13, 14, 15, 16)

Controlling Operating Profit (Ref. 17, 18, 19, 20, 21)

What is Operating Profit?
It is the profit before deductions for interest and income tax, and before any extraordinary gains and losses. Operating profit is sometimes called EBIT: Earnings Before Interest and Tax. It is a direct measure of how well the management managed the resources under their control.

Turning sales revenue into operating profit is the priority aim of a management team.

Need for a Clear, Practical Focus
Too often management reports contain too much detail. A management team needs a simple formula that contains the critical factors effecting operating profit, and by monitoring this formula the management team can focus its efforts to ensure operating profit is maintained and increased.

A management team needs a simple formula whereby it orientates itself to its priority aim. Each person in the management team needs to have a clearly defined responsibility for one or several lines in the formula or even just a part of one line. The summary formula is then supported by detailed reports whereby managers review the performance of the teams and determine necessary action. The Profit Profile (Ref.17) provides the necessary formula.

The Profit Profile and Operating Profit (Ref 17)

Sales Price	100%
Product Cost	50%
Variable Expenses	12%
Gross Profit	38%
Fixed Expenses	28%
Operating Profit 10%	

Operating profit is the small difference between two much larger numbers, sales revenue and expenses. Small changes in either have much larger impact on operating profit.

Exercise: In the diagram below, the current ratios are shown as percentages. The second column shows the changes effected by a 1% increase in sales and a 1% decrease in each of the three expenses. Complete a similar exercise with the ratios for your own business.

	Current ratios	*1 % change*
Sales	100	101
Product cost	50	49.5
Variable expenses	12	11.88
Gross margin	38	39.62
Fixed expenses	28	27.72
Operating profit	10	11.9

24

A 1% sales revenue increase combined with a 1% expenses decrease produces a 19% improvement in operating profit.

Not Just Historical Review

It is not enough for management teams to review historical performance via the formula. They also need a means of projecting the effects on operating profit of planned and unplanned changes in the factors effecting operating profits. The profit profile provides this proactive planning tool.

A Simple Example

Suppose we are running a fast foods van. We sell a range of products with the average sales revenue of £15.00 per litre. The product costs £4.00 per litre. There are variable expenses – spoons, napkins, straws and toppings – of £1.00 per litre. We have a sales volume of 5,000 litres. Our fixed expenses – petrol, depreciation, repairs and maintenance, mobile phone, insurance – are £30,000 per year (These figures ignore goods and services and other value added taxes)

Profit margin per unit – the key to operating profit		Calculating operating profit	
Sales revenue per litre	£15.00	Profit margin	£10.00
Product cost	£4.00	Sales volume	5,000 litres
Variable expenses	£1.00	Total profit margin	£50,000
Profit margin per litre	£10.00	Fixed expenses	£30,000
		Operating profit	£20,000
Profit margin/ unit is the essential starting point for building sustainable operating profit.		The essential steps are to multiply the sales margin by the sales volume.	

Calculate the break-even

The break-even is the volume of sales need to cover the fixed expenses. This can be obtained by dividing the fixed expenses by the profit margin per litre, that is: £30,000/£10 = 3,000 litres

Allocation of Fixed Costs or Overheads

A second method of calculating operating profit is to allocate fixed costs to each unit sold. In the example, £30,000 allocated over 5,000 litres is £6.00 per litre. We can then calculate operating profit by calculating the operating profit per litre, (£10.00 less £6.00 gives £4.00) multiplied by sales volume.

In this introduction we will not consider overhead allocation methods. The types of problems that occur are well illustrated by our van business. For example, a sundae takes more time, effort and so on than a single cone; should it be allocated more overhead or not? Throughout this book series, overhead will be treated as a burden on the business to be recovered by profit margin per unit multiplied by sales volume. break-even is defined as the point at which this formula equals overhead costs.

Simple Concepts Well Applied

Being able to understand, analyse and manipulate the basics of operating profit is important. Not being able to is like a marketing manager not understanding positioning or an accountant not knowing the difference between debt and equity.

The concept promoted here is to create insightful, simple concepts and apply them constantly, thoroughly.

Profit Sensitivity (Ref 17)

The profit profile contains a summary of the factors that have most impact on profit. It can now be used to assess the effect on operating profit to planned and unplanned changes. In the following examples the factors are varied one at a time. This seldom happens – normally a change in costs affects price which affects volume. Changes in several variables are analysed in the following sections. We will continue to use the van business example.

The Profit Profile

		Per unit	Total
Annual break-even volume			3,000 litres
Annual sales volume			5,000 litres
Sales revenue		£15.00	£75,000
Less:	Product code	£4.00	£209,000
	Variable expenses	£1.00	£15,000
Equals:	Profit margin	£10.00	£50,000
Less:	Fixed expenses		£30,000
Equals:	Operating profit		**£20,000**

Notes:

1. Includes break-even and sales volumes not included in conventional incomes statements

2. Variable expenses are separated

3. Per unit values are included

4. It is quick and easy to update

5. It keeps attention focused on the critical factors that most impact on profits

6. It is a simple format that provides a focus for the whole management team.

7. It avoids too much detail and so guides the management team to make the best decisions on profit maintenance.

10% Sales Volume Increase

Only items that change are shown in the 'changes' column of the Profit Profile.

		Before		Changes
Annual break-even volume		3,000 litres		
Annual sales volume		5,000 litres		540 litres
		Per unit	Total	Total
Sales revenue		£15.00	£75,000	£7,500
Less:	Product costs	£4.00	£20,000	£2,000
	Variable expenses	£1.00	£5,000	£500
Equals:	Profit margin	£10.00	£50,000	£5,000
Less:	Fixed expenses		£30,000	
Equals:	Operating profit		**£20,000**	**£5,000**

The main question raised here is whether the business has the production capacity to handle such an increase in volume. To deal with this question we can adjust the profit profile and add "capacity volume" which is defined as the volume able to be produced without altering fixed expenses.

10% Sales Price Increase

		Before		Changes	
Capacity volume		6,000			
Break-even volume		3,000		-391	
Sales volume		5,000			
	Per unit	Total		Per unit	Total
Sales revenue	£15.00	£75,000.00		£1.50	£7,500.00
Less: Product costs	£4.00	£20,000.00			
Variable expenses	£1.00	£5,000.00			
Equals: Profit margin	£10.00	£50,000.00		£1.50	£7,500.00
Less: Fixed expenses		£30,000.00			
Equals: Operating profit		£20,000.00			£7,500.00

With the price increase, there is a noticeably greater impact than the volume increase. That is because the sales price increase improves the profit margin per unit. As a result, the break-even is decreased. Managers know these relationships, but too often forget the magnitude of the swings in operating profit resulting from quite small changes in profit margin per unit.

In this example, the operating profit increased 37.5% from a 10% increase in profit margin. It follows that every 1% improvement in profit margin increases operating profit 3.75%.

How would your shareholders react to a 4% increase in profits over budget?

Do you know the sensitivity of your business to the types of changes above?

How sharply are you and the management team focused on the art of the possible?

How committed are you to achieving best possible?

28

Understanding the Multiplier Effect of Changes on Operating Profit

A 10% increase in volume produced a 25% increase in operating profit. Why? This is because the profit margin for the first 3,000 litres merely covered fixed expenses. Above break-even, the total profit margin per unit becomes operating profit. Thus the percentage increase in operating profit reflects the percentage increase above break-even, not the percentage increase in overall volume.

Managers instinctively understand these issues but frequently overlook the magnitude of potential changes to operating profit. Intensity and focus tend to diminish as sales stretch beyond break-even, where in fact intensity and focus should increase because every sale above break-even has a multiplier effect on profits.

This multiplier does not operate as dramatically in all businesses. This will be illustrated by analysing our van business. Managers need to understand the multiplier effects for their own business

10% Product Cost Increase

	Before		Changes	
Capacity volume		6,000		
Break-even volume		3,000	+125 litres	
Sales volume		5,000		
	Per unit	Total	Per unit	Total
Sales revenue	£15.00	£75,000.00		
Less: Product costs	£4.00	£20,000.00	(£0.4)	(£2,000)
Variable expenses	£1.00	£5,000.00		
Equals: Profit margin	£10.00	£50,000.00	(£0.4)	(£2,000)
Less: Fixed expenses		£30,000.00		
Equals: Operating profit		**£20,000.00**		**(£2,000)**

Profit falls 10% in line with an increase of 10% in costs.

Exercise:

1. Calculate the impact of a 10% product cost decrease.
2. Calculate the impact of a 10% increase in:
   (a) variable expenses (b) fixed expenses.

29

Summary

For a product based business:

1. A sales price change has a much greater effect than a sales volume change.

2. Both sales price and volume changes have a multiplier effect on operating profit.

3. Product cost, variable and fixed expense changes have the same percentage effect on operating profit.

Applying the Profit Profile to Different Businesses (Ref 17)

Every Business is the Same but Different

Managers and management teams typically believe their business to be different. They are right in the same sense that every person is different, but we all eat, breathe and have relationships.

The profit profile focuses on the basics and reflects how well the management has applied itself to the priority aim of converting sales revenue into operating profit.

Must Understand the Niche

Within any industry, there are certain success factors common to all businesses; but each business places different emphasis on each factor. For example, in food retailing the factors include price, service level and store style or presentation. A full service supermarket blends these elements one way while a discount warehouse market chooses another pattern.

The profit profile reflects the success of management in implementing these different operational philosophies.

Internal Creative Focus

The profit profile provides a tool to focus work teams on what they can do to influence the factors in the profit profile so that operating is improved.

Sales Revenue Variable Costs

Not all variable costs are related to volume. There are variable costs which are related to sales revenue. These include discounts, commissions and rebates. Variable expenses may need to be split in the profit profile.

Retailers and Wholesalers

The product cost is the cost of purchase of the goods. Variable costs could include ticketing, discounts and sales prices, and the cost of electronic security devices attached to products. Typically, retailers and wholesalers operate on a mark-up system, with product cost being a major factor in the profit profile.

Service Businesses

The main differences with a service business are as follows.

- Product cost is much lower than for other businesses.
- There are high fixed costs
- Variable costs can be on both volume and revenue – for example, sales discount and the cost of soap, towels and bathrobes in a hotel.
- Sales volume is expressed as a % of capacity – % of seats filled on an airline or rooms in a hotel

10% Volume Increase – Service Business Profit Profile

	Before	Changes
Sales volume % of capacity	80%	10%
Sales revenue	£500,000	£50,000
Variable expenses		
Sales	(£30,000)	(£3,000)
Sales volume	(£15,000)	(£1,500)
Product cost	(£20,000)	(£2,000)
Profit margin	£435,000	£43,500
Fixed expenses	360000	
Operating profit	£75,000	£43,500

Exercise:

1. Calculate the effect of a 10% price increase.

Calculating break-even for service business

The break-even for a service business is calculated in the same way as for a product-based business but based on each percentage point of capacity. In the "Service Business Profit Profile" example above, we can calculate the profit margin on each percentage point of capacity.

Service Business Break-even

	Per % point
Sales revenue	£6,250
Variable expenses	
Sales £	(£300)
Sales volume	(£150)
Product cost	(£200)
Profit margin	£5,600

Therefore the break-even capacity is 64.3%. (It takes 64.3% of capacity to cover the fixed expenses of £360,000)

Profit Sensitivity of service business

For a service business with low product cost, a volume increase has almost as much effect as a price increase. This is in contrast to product based businesses where a price increase has a much greater impact on operating profit than a volume increase.

These differences become important in the following section on strategies and tactics.

Manufacturing Product Cost

The product cost for manufacturers must be calculated. It is the central focus of the factory or operations team in a manufacturing business.

Manufacturing Cost Profile

Practical capacity	12,000 units	
Actual output	10,000 units	
	Total	**Per unit**
Raw materials	£1,000,000	£100.00
Packaging	£150,000	£15.00
Direct labour	£1,500,000	£150.00
Variable overhead	£300,000	£30.00
Fixed overhead	£1,600,000	£160.00
Total manufacturing cost	£4,550,000	£455.00

Notes

1. The output potential capacity is the output potential without further investment or without increasing fixed overheads

2. Product cost per unit is a calculated amount and depends on accurate information on costs and output.

3. The cost per unit is an average cost involving only manufacturing costs

Idle Capacity Cost

In the previous example, fixed overhead is distributed over actual output giving £160 per unit. The idle capacity (2000 units) is acknowledged as a sales opportunity. It is accepted that the fixed costs may be spread over the practical product capacity. If so, the Manufacturing Cost Profile would need to show "Idle Capacity Cost" – this cost however is not necessarily controllable by the manufacturing team.

Multiple products

Total manufacturing costs can be aggregated across many products to give the averaged costs of the manufacturing unit. Alternatively the manufacturing cost profile can be applied to each product line. Where this is done, care must be taken in allocating fixed manufacturing costs. Any such allocation can only be arbitrary. What is preferred is to treat each product as providing a contribution to manufacturing fixed overhead.

To create a profit profile for each product line, the manufacturing overhead can be allocated; this is best done using some common denominator such as direct labour or materials. Based on such allocations, product lines can appear unprofitable and great care needs to be taken lest inappropriate decisions be made.

Product Line Profit Profile

	Economy	Standard	Deluxe	Average/ Totals
Sales price	£50.00	£60.00	£70.00	£58.33
Product cost	(£28.50)	(£35.50)	(£38.00)	(£33.58)
Variable expense	(£3.00)	(£5.00)	(£7.00)	(£4.67)
Profit margin/ unit	£18.50	£19.50	£25.00	£20.08
Sales volume	20,000	30,000	10,000	50,000
Total profit margin	£370,000	£585,000	£250,000	£1,205,000
Fixed expenses		(£8,450,000)		
Operating profit		£360,000		

Notes:

1. It is often helpful to show percentages in this report.

2. Manufacturing fixed overheads is not allocated across products but is treated as part of fixed operating expenses.

Because product is capitalised as inventory, it is important to know accurately which costs are classified product costs.

Turnaround (Ref. 17)
Profit Profile for Turnaround

Sales volume		60,000
Break-even volume		73,400
Capacity volume		80,000
	Per unit	**Total**
Sales revenue	£40.00	£2,400,000
Product cost	(£26.00)	(£1,560,000)
Variable cost	(£8.00)	(£480,000)
Profit margin	£6.00	£360,000
Fixed expenses		(£440,000)
Operating profit (loss)		(£80,000)

Analysis

1. Fixed expenses at 18% of revenue are high. If this was the division of a large business, and an element of fixed expense was allocated, this would need to be reviewed. Each element of fixed expenses needs to be reviewed.

2. Break-even is 91.75% of total capacity. This is also very high.

3. Even at 100% of capacity the operating profit will only be £40,000 (£6 x 80,000 units – fixed expenses) or 1.7% of sales. This is very low.

Actions

It is possible to correct the situation by loading all the necessary improvements onto one factor such as sales price or a reduction in advertising. This type of corrective action usually distorts the business and may jeopardise the business in the long term. The price increase necessary to generate an operating profit of £100,000 assuming no change in volume is £43 or a 7.5% price increase. This is large and could certainly effect volume.

A balanced approach to the turnaround is preferable. Below is the profit profile for a 1% improvement in all of the key factors.

One Percent Improvement in each Profit Margin Factor

Sales volume				60,000
Break-even volume				73,400
Capacity volume				80,000

	Before per unit	Per unit	Total	Changes
Sales revenue	£40.00	£40.40	£2,424,000	£24,000
Product cost	(£26.00)	(£25.74)	(£154,400)	£15,600
Variable cost	(£8.00)	(£7.92)	(£475,200)	(£4,800)
Fixed expenses			(£435,600)	£4,400
Operating profit (loss)			(£31,200)	£48,800

Each 1% improvement increases operating profit by £48,800. Therefore a 4% improvement in each of the factors will improve operating profit by £195,200 and turn the loss (£80,000) into a profit of £115,200. The key aim of the management team in this turnaround must be to improve the profit margin per unit to at least £8, preferable £10.

Exercise: Calculate the percentage changes you would need to make to produce an operating profit of £150,000.

Controlling Profit Erosion (Ref. 17)

Sales Factors

Rebates, discounts, coupons
- Are discounts built into your computer pricing?
- When were they last reviewed?
- Does your sales team give discounts in units of 5%, 10%?
- Can they be guided to offer 2%, 4%?
- Can each of your salespeople identify ten clients where discounts could be reduced without loss of volume?

- Can your sales team be guided to sell the benefits and retain margin?

Product Cost

Waste, rework, repairs, shrinkage
- Are losses and waste accurately recorded?
- Are the main problem areas identified?
- What actions would reduce waste and rework by 25%?
- How can warranties and returns be reduced 50%?
- How can recalls be eliminated?

Administration

Lost discounts, misinformation
- What costs are incurred due to wrong or incomplete information?
- Do you ever lose out on volume or prompt payment discounts?
- Do debtors ever hold up payments because of errors in invoices or packing advices?

Strategies and Tactics

Using the Profit Profile to Assess the Impact of Changes on Operating Profit
The commercial environment is not static. Competitive pressures increase, raw materials increase in price, some competitors become vulnerable.

- Should we drop prices to gain market share ?
- Should we increase price? How much volume could we stand to use?
- Should the product cost increase be passed on? How can we assess potential effects?

The Profit Profile can be used to Explore "What if...." questions.

Care is required in estimating the volume change as a consequence of any price change.

Actions supporting this judgement could include :

• team brainstorming with all managers, or sales staff

• questionnaires to customers

• formal market research

Three issues will now be examined.

Tactic 1.   Decrease in sales price to gain volume
Tactic 2.   Increase in sales price with a loss of volume
Tactic 3.   Passing on a materials cost increase with a loss of volume

Tactic 1: Decrease price, gain volume

This is a bad idea for product-based businesses. Typically the increase in volume has to be very large to offset even a modest price drop. The reason is that the small drop in sales price becomes a large decrease in profit margin per unit.

The management team in a product based business needs to protect profit margin per unit and NOT give it away.

Service businesses suffer much less. There is a small drop in profits, so the risk of gaining the extra volume to increase profits is possibly justified. Even so, the move needs to be supported by a careful analysis of where the new business will come from – customer by customer – and preferably tried first with several customers.

10% Sales Price Decrease with 10% Sales Volume Increase

Product Business

	Before		After	
Break-even volume	36,700		55,000	
Sales volume	60,000		66,000	

	Per unit	Total	Per unit	Total
Sales revenue	£40.00	£2,400,000	£36.00	£2,376,000
Product cost	(£22.00)	(£1,320,000)	(£22.00)	(£1,452,000)
Variable expenses	(£6.00)	(£360,000)	(£6.00)	(£396,000)
Profit margin	£12.00	£720,000	£8.00	£528,000
Fixed expenses		(£440,000)		(£440,000)
Operating profit		£280,000		£88,000

Exercise: Calculate the volume increase needed to offset the 10% price decrease

Answer: At the new profit margin per unit of £8, the volume would need to be 90,000 units to generate the £720,000 of total profit margin.

Service Business

	Before	After
Volume as % of capacity	80%	88%
Sales revenue	£2,080,000	£2,059,200
Product cost	(£80,000)	(£88,000)
Variable expenses	(£120,000)	(£132,000)
Profit margin	£1,880,000	£1,839,200
Fixed expenses	(£1,600,000)	(£1,600,000)
Operating profit	£280,000	£239,200

Note: Each percentage point was worth £26,000, but is now worth £23,400, thus reducing revenue (at 88%) to £2,059,200

Tactic 2: Increase price, lose volume

This is a good idea for product businesses. The increased profit comes from the large increase in profit margin per unit. But how many companies will give up volume to become more profitable? Most sales managers wouldn't hear of it. There are a host of side benefits –

for example the company gets more focused on core clients; service improves; quality improves; and morale improves. Growth can then again proceed based on strong word of mouth.

This tactic is not effective in service businesses unless the drop in volume enables a reduction in fixed expenses.

10% Sales Price Increase with 10% Sales Volume Decrease

Product Business

	Before		After	
Break-even volume	36,700		27,500	
Sales volume	60,000		54,000	

	Per unit	Total	Per unit	Total
Sales revenue	£40.00	£2,400,000	£44.00	£2,376,000
Product cost	(£22.00)	(£1,320,000)	(£22.00)	(£1,188,000)
Variable expenses	(£6.00)	(£360,000)	(£6.00)	(£324,000)
Profit margin	£12.00	£720,000	£16.00	£864,000
Fixed expenses		(£440,000)		(£440,000)
Operating profit		£280,000		£424,000

Exercise: Calculate the decrease needed to offset the 10% increase in price

Answer: At the new profit margin per unit of £16, the volume would need fall to 45,000 units to generate the £720,000 of total profit margin.

Service Business

	Before	After
Volume as % of capacity	80%	88%
Sales revenue	£2,080,000	£2,059,200
Product cost	(£80,000)	(£72,000)
Variable expenses	(£120,000)	(£108,000)
Profit margin	£1,880,000	£1,879,200
Fixed expenses	(£1,600,000)	(£1,600,000)
Operating profit	£280,000	£279,200

Note: New percentage volume value £286,000 per point

Service businesses: The action is in revenue and fixed expenses. If revenue can be increased without losing volume or increasing fixed expenses, then profits will improve dramatically.

41

Tactic 3 Product Cost Increase – Pass On or Not?

A 10% Product Cost Increase Passed On to Customers with an 8% Decrease in Volume

	Product Business			
	Before		**After**	
Break-even volume	36,700		36,700	
Sales volume	60,000		55,200	
	Per unit	**Total**	**Per unit**	**Total**
Sales revenue	£40.00	£2,400,000	£42.20	£2,329,440
Product cost	(£22.00)	(£1,320,000)	(£24.20)	(£1,335,840)
Variable expenses	(£6.00)	(£360,000)	(£6.00)	(£331,200)
Profit margin	£12.00	£720,000	£12.00	£662,400
Fixed expenses		(£440,000)		(£440,000)
Operating profit		£280,000		£222,400

Note: This analysis is the same as for a price increase with volume reduction

Establish the profit profile of your business
(1)

	Per unit	Total
Capacity volume (2)		
Sales volume (3)		
Sales volume as % of capacity (3)		
Break-even volume (4)		
Sales revenue		
Product cost		
Raw materials (5)		
Consumables		
Direct labour		
Manufacturing variable cost		
Total product cost		
Variable operating expenses		
Profit margin		
Fixed expenses		
Operating (6)		
Manufacturing		
Operating profit		

Notes:
1. Use only those lines appropriate for your business.
2. This is the volume available without plant changes or increase in fixed costs.

3. Use one or the other depending on whether product or service type business.
4. This can be expressed as % of capacity for service businesses.
5. This can be in a separate, supporting reports.
6. Manufacturing cost profile report.
7. This can be in separate, supporting reports.

Questions:

1. What % volume is break-even?
2. Is it low enough?
3. Is the profit to sales ratio high enough?
4. What is a good industry standard?
5. What factors are eroding profits?
   - discounts and rebates
   - waste
   - rework and poor quality
   - misinformation
   - other ...

Assessing Sensitivity and Key Trade Offs

If necessary, do a Profit Profile to establish profit margins for each product group. Then add total profit margin for each product group to get company total profit margin

1. Calculate decreasing product cost 5%, increasing prices 1% and decreasing fixed cost 5%.

	Before		After	
Capacity volume (2)				
Sales volume (3)				
Sales volume as % of capacity (3)				
Break-even volume (4)				
	Per unit	Total	Per unit	Total
Sales revenue				
Product cost				
Raw materials (5)				
Consumables				
Direct labour				
Manufacturing variable cost				
Total product cost				
Variable operating expenses				
Profit margin				
Fixed expenses				
Operating (6)				
Manufacturing				
Operating profit				

2. Calculate decreasing prices 5% while increasing volume 5%

	Before	After
Capacity volume (2)		
Sales volume (3)		
Sales volume as % of capacity (3)		
Break-even volume (4)		

	Per unit	Total	Per unit	Total
Sales revenue				
Product cost				
Raw materials (5)				
Consumables				
Direct labour				
Manufacturing variable cost				
Total product cost				
Variable operating expenses				
Profit margin				
Fixed expenses				
Operating (6)				
Manufacturing				
Operating profit				

46

3. Calculate increasing prices 5% while decreasing volume 5%

	Before		After	
Capacity volume (2)				
Sales volume (3)				
Sales volume as % of capacity (3)				
Break-even volume (4)				
	Per unit	**Total**	**Per unit**	**Total**
Sales revenue				
Product cost				
Raw materials (5)				
Consumables				
Direct labour				
Manufacturing variable cost				
Total product cost				
Variable operating expenses				
Profit margin				
Fixed expenses				
Operating (6)				
Manufacturing				
Operating profit				

4. Calculate the practical changes that will increase operating profit 25%.

Don't load too much on any single factor; keep the business in balance. Use your judgement to assess changes you believe are practical. The increase of 25% to be over and above your 'best estimate' of the profit for the current year. The increase to be achieved without capital expenditure.

	Before		After	
Capacity volume (2)				
Sales volume (3)				
Sales volume as % of capacity (3)				
Break-even volume (4)				
	Per unit	Total	Per unit	Total
Sales revenue				
Product cost				
Raw materials (5)				
Consumables				
Direct labour				
Manufacturing variable cost				
Total product cost				
Variable operating expenses				
Profit margin				
Fixed expenses				
Operating (6)				
Manufacturing				
Operating profit				

Identifying Likely Projects

From your notes and analyses identify the six projects that would achieve an increase in operating profit of at least 25%. Identify those projects under your direct control.

Project	Action/comment
1	
2	
3	
4	
5	
6	

The Business Growth Spread Sheet

A budget is the core of any business planning. It should portray a conservative, realistic expectation of what will happen. It needs to be quite detailed, representing the thinking out of the details of the business operations and the financial consequences of those operations.

The details in a budget are at once its strength and its weakness. Too often I find management teams bogged in the detail, and not retaining enough of an overview, too lost in working in the business and with not enough focus of working on the business. For this reason I have developed the business growth spread sheet. The spreadsheet is in three sections as shown below.

The budget or best estimate of the result for the current financial year	The summary of the projects to be implemented and the effect on the profit profile factors this financial year and the next financial year.	The target for this financial year as a result of the projects and the flow-on effect of the projects into the next financial year.

The concept assumes achievement of the budget as the base. The projects are then those activities selected by the management team whereby the team aims to add momentum to the business this year with a flow on effect into next year.

Business Growth Plan for

Profit profile	Budget or best estimate		Projects and their effects	Years						Projected after-effect of projects	
	Opening			Current year effects			Year 1 effects			Current year	Year 1
	£		Sales Projects	Sales £	Costs £		Sales £	Costs £		£	£
Revenue			1	£	£		£	£			
			2	£	£		£	£			
			3	£	£		£	£			
			4	£	£		£	£			
			Total sales change	£			£				
			Direct costs change from sales projects		£			£			
Direct costs			Direct cost projects								
			1		£			£			
			2		£			£			
			3		£			£			
			4		£			£			
			Total direct cost changes		£			£			
Gross profit											
Overheads			Overhead projects								
			1		£			£			
			2		£			£			
			3		£			£			
			4		£			£			
			Total overhead changes		£			£			
Operating profit											
% gross profit	%									%	%
% profit to sales	%									%	%
£ increase in profit											

There are two crucial questions about the budget that forms the basis for this spreadsheet. (1) How is the budget set? (2) What happens if the team gets into the year and finds it is behind budget?

The budget is set with the central idea in mind that a business is like a fly wheel – it has a certain existing inertia not that difficult to keep going. So the budget for next financial year could begin with this year's result then be increased or decreased based on projected economic activity and projected competitor activity. So, for example, the budget might be a 3% growth in revenues over last year, no significant increase in overheads, and with the same margin giving a 6% increase in operating profit. This is of course quite modest, but reflects the momentum of the business. Now, the management team reviews the projects, selects those offering the best pay-back this year and with strong flow on into next year. This then increases revenue growth to 12%, with a improvement in margin and a reduction in overheads through better use of technology resulting in better business processes giving a 32% increase in operating profit.

Ensuring budget achievement

When a management team finds that the base budget is not being achieved, then it needs to quickly identify additional projects designed to recover the budget. The budget is the base, the projects then add momentum to the business to improve upon this base. It is important that the projects designed and agreed to add momentum are not then used to fill the hole in the budget, because then the management team has added no momentum to the business. A management team adopting this philosophy will very likely be in a state of 'nervous self-belief'. This as it should be for any team or individual committing him or herself to superior performance.

It is common for a management team adopting this philosophy to find ways for the business to achieve more revenue without significant increase in overhead and in part, this results from the management team itself being more effective at doing that which it needs to do. In simple terms, the cost of the management team remains constant while the revenue and profits increase. Almost invariably the emotional state of such teams is one of energy and excitement.

Challenges are faced and beaten – there is much nervous energy, pressure and stress. It is great when the result is achieved. For the directors overseeing such teams, it is crucial that they understand the strain of achievement and the potential for burnout from prolonged exposure to the energy of challenge and insist that all team members take an annual vacation of at least two weeks enabling complete revitalisation.

A strategy template

The business growth spreadsheet enables focus on those activities most adding to the bottom line. Typically, the base of the business is managed in a regular, steady manner while the projects receive 'extra focus and attention'. The spreadsheet was never intended as a strategy development document. However, by assessing the flow on of projects, the process enables projection of the business over two years and frequently I find that this is sufficient forward projection and no further strategic thinking need be done.

Each year, the budget is set based on last year and adjusted based on the estimate of economic and competitor activity, then the projects selected to add momentum and to improve operating profit, so that each year the management team does a two year strategic review. This is made more effective by ensuring a 'zero base' for all projects, that is any projects begun last year and not yet completed are then put in priority with all possible projects and may or may not become a priority for the coming year.

When using the spreadsheet this way, capital expenditure projects can be added, as can long term projects. For example, the decision to invest now in e-commerce knowing that this will increase overheads without commensurate increase in revenues or profits for two or maybe three or more years. For the purpose of annual accounts, long-term project expenditure would most likely be written off in the year incurred. For the purposes of the management team, long-term project expenditure should perhaps be shown as profits reinvested in an accumulating fund, and that eventually the team is expected to recover this fund and to show returns on the capital in the fund.

Business processes

When reviewing expense-based projects it is important to have a clear, simple model of the business in mind. What should be avoided are projects involving review of the list of expenses and cutting £100 there and £2,000 here and ...

The focus should be on the business processes. Imagine the business processes as a series of pipes and all the materials, product, information and movement of people is through these pipes. The expenses are a consequence of this movement and of the nature and shape of the pipes, so alter the pipes and the expenses will change. For example, imagine a customer services unit of ten people, responding to customers, taking orders and so on. An expense review might uncover some several thousand pounds in lost time and inefficient use of mobile phones, etc. Realising these savings will inevitably be difficult, generating resentment for 'pettiness' among the team. Detailed investigation of customer inquiries however might show that 40% involve queries about product – static information that customers themselves could research if the product information was on the internet – and that 60% of the team's time is devoted to such inquiries. An investment of say £100,000 to improve the product information on the world wide web could then result in a permanent reduction of two or even three in the team with an increase in focus and service. These results ignore any inefficiencies or misuse of mobile phones, all of which could easily be seen as 'perks' by team members.

A good starting point for identifying opportunities for improving business processes is to identify the hassles encountered by team members in their job, especially those that recur, then identifying the hassles encountered by customers. Most likely underlying a recurring hassle is a business process that could usefully be fixed so that the hassle does not occur, and simultaneously taking advantage to improve the outputs associated with the business process.

Identifying good profit to sales ratios

Recently, when prospecting for new clients I have been privileged to encounter two extremely well run businesses. I relate these anecdotes because of their effect on me. In short, these companies altered my view of what is a 'good result' and what is a 'great result'. Unfortunately I am not able to name the companies concerned, so you will have to accept my word that they exist.

The first company is in the newspaper industry, producing and distributing a number of local newspapers. Revenues are some £30 million, with investments in plant of some £20 million. The profit to sales ratio is 31%. When initially told this number I was incredulous, but was shown information that confirmed it. The second business is in the foundry industry. It has revenues of £3 million, with profit to sales of 30%. These are excellent results by any standard. How did they do it?

Both managing directors were quite willing to discuss how they achieved these results. The remarkable thing is that there is no great secret and certainly you will know all that is needed to do the same in your business. Both managing directors had a clear focus on business processes and the need to keep refining and improving those processes. In neither instance, were there high levels of technology involved. The focus was on correctly confronting every hassle when it occurred, and on involving the staff in finding and implementing the best possible solution. Both managers said that their staff in any section could tell me of the key business processes in that section, as well as the hassles and what was being done about them. With those profit to sales ratios I believed them. The foundry business could show me the book where every problem or hassle for the last ten years was recorded, with notes on what was done and who did it. Neither managing director was 'charismatic', but both shared a simple, focused discipline of daily identifying things to improve the operation of their business and clearly exhibited the day by day patience and discipline to do the few simple things they saw would add up to a better bottom line. The smoother the business process and the more the people understand and can implement them the fewer people you need and the more they can do.

You can do the same in your business. But it is not a 'quick fix'. The starting point is for you and your team members to begin and to quietly, patiently and progressively improve your profit to sales by implementing the tactics and philosophy outlined in these books.

Case study examples

Below are examples illustrating application of the ideas. All of the businesses showed improvements in operating profit and in the profit to sales ratio over periods ranging from four or five months to eighteen months. In all cases, the delay in results showing in the profit and loss figures was due to the rate at which the management team mastered the art of maintaining sufficient effective focus on the core of the business (to ensure budget) while generating extra focus and effort on the two or three projects to add momentum. The second important point is that the improvement in results did not always emerge from the projects nominated – that is, the team began with what it thought were the priority projects only to find that improved results popped out somewhere else, usually related to the beginning project. A consistent issue was keeping down the number of projects being worked on at any time. One is okay, three is hard and four is impossible. But it does depend on the nature of the project.

The final key point is for the top team to conceptualise what to implement within a project – that is, to identify the precise steps and who has to do them. Consistently I find that this exercise is left too general, and people are asked not only to act in a way most likely to achieve the result, but also to create their own concepts of what those actions should be. This vagueness is usually too much to ask and the result will be disappointing.

The principle guiding the identification of the actions most likely to achieve the result is that for every goal there are behaviours that must be acted out. It is the task of the management team to think out the actions that are most likely to achieve the result – this is a crucial part of the planning process. By getting behaviours clear, then the leadership team can guide people to do the things most likely to facilitate success, and to ensure an effective balance of the actions that maintain momentum (achieving budget) and then add to that momentum (focused, selective growth or profit development). This is well illustrated in the first case study. (See *The Five Steps to Effective Business Leadership* for a more detailed discussion on this issue.)

Case 1: Improving profitability in industrial products sales and distribution

This company had been a client for eight or ten years. For each of the last four years, we had implemented the philosophy above with management team workshops, usually of two days, in which the agreed forecast for the coming financial year was reviewed and projects identified to add profits. The first year had been a learning year for the team, and the results, while apparent, had not been spectacular. The second year was to have been expansive, but then came the Asian crisis, which was not predicted, and the comment made by the managing director was 'the projects saved the result'. The third year was very sound, but the focus had been on cost reduction because the economic climate was tight and had been predicted to be so. The year illustrated here is predicted to be quite expansive, in fact this is forecast for the coming two or three years. Therefore the team is now focused on growth and market share. The spreadsheet is below, the workshop was conducted two months before the commencement of the new financial year but after the budget had been agreed by the directors.

Business Growth Plan for ..... Industrial products distributor — Years 2000/2001

Budget or best estimate		Projects and their effects	Current year effects		Year 1 effects		Projected after-effect of projects	
Profit profile	Opening	£ Sales Projects	Sales	Costs	Sales	Costs	Current year £	Year 1 £
Revenue	£9,700,000	1 Process equipment, new product line	£200,000	£100,000	£350,000	£190,000		
		2 OEM producers	£150,000	£75,000	£250,000	£130,000		
		3 Key accounts and target clients	£260,000	£130,000	£350,000	£160,000		
		4 Improving service, improving stock accuracy	£100,000	£50,000	£250,000	£130,000		
		Total sales change			£1,200,000			
		Direct costs change from sales projects		£335,000		£635,000	£10,410,000	£11,610,000
Direct costs	£4,753,000	Direct cost projects						
		1	£	£	£	£		
		2	£	£	£	£		
		3	£	£	£	£		
		4	£	£	£	£		
		Total direct cost changes		£335,000		£635,000	£5,108,000	£5,743,000
Gross profit	£4,947,000						£5,302,000	£5,867,000
Overheads	£3,735,000	Overhead projects						
		1 Allow for overhead ascalation		£115,000		£		
		2		£		£		
		3		£		£		
		4		£		£		
		Total overhead changes		£115,000		£	£3,735,000	£3,850,000
Operating profit	£1,212,000						£1,567,000	£2,017,000
% gross profit	% 51.00						% 50.93	% 50.53
% profit to sales	% 12.49						% 15.05	% 17.37
£ increase in profit							£355,000	£805,000

Below are the notes that were circulated with the spreadsheet after the meeting. There are two crucial points to note: (1) the clear and firm separation between regional managers focused on sales and the MD and rest of the management team focused on improving service; (2) the way in which the sales team is focused to ensure the best possible chance of achieving the focused growth.

Notes as agreed

1. Spread sheet attached. The strategic philosophy embodied is to secure market share over the next two or three years, while allowing some gradual easing of margins. Margin pressure to come from (1) product increasingly a commodity. (2) Internationally available pricing from the internet.

2. If the team focuses on and achieves the results as presented in the spreadsheet over the coming two years, this would be a significant consolidation of the business in its market.

3. Major effort to be placed on improving customer service as this will become the key point of differentiation. This thrust to be lead by MD. For example, deal finally with stock accuracy.

4. Regional managers to focus and be facilitated to focus on market share and sales team effectiveness.

5. Key coaching issues for regional managers summarised as follows.

✓ Sales people must be guided to see where growth can come from.

✓ Must not present growth in terms of simple percentage.

✓ Must focus on the behaviours most likely to achieve result.

✓ Example; consider a sales territory as below.

✓ This type of analysis needs to be done for every territory, then all salespeople will 'see' clearly how to achieve the best possible result in their territory.

✓ The sales growth for the business can then arise by adding the results for each territory. BUT I REPEAT IT NEEDS TO BE DONE AS OUTLINED BELOW. OTHERWISE THIS SORT OF TARGETED GROWTH WILL NOT OCCUR.

Territory No 1	Revenue	Comment on behaviour needed
Sales last year 1999	£270,000	Taken as the base
Allow 2.5% growth	£6,750	Needs regular calling, good service and delivery, conscientious pursuing of opportunities
Process equipment sales 1999 were £2000. Target 2000 is £20,000.	£20,000	Need to identify likely customers where we can make extra sales without making an additional call on someone else. Regular and focused calling. Find out what they use and then pursue some or all of the business. Target to secure the sales from eight accounts.
OEM, key accounts and target clients –selecting and focusing on a few most likely to offer good sales increase. Last year a 30% increase from those accounts was targeted. This year, target eight accounts with last-year revenues of £80,000. Seek an increase this year of £15,000 or an 18.75% increase, which is less than the gains achieved last year.	£15,000	Need focused and effective calling, setting goals and targets for each of the eight selected accounts.
Total sales target 2000	**£311,750**	**This is a 15.5% increase over last year. As such, it looks hard but each of the specific and targeted behaviours is realistic and the result achievable.**

Summary of behaviours needed are:

  a. Regular calling on all clients with focus and purpose to ensure service and to secure additional business.

  b. Intensive, focused calling on process valve prospects. Likely no more than eight targets.

  c. Intensive focused calling on OEM or target clients or key accounts. Likely no more than eight targets.

6. The tone within the Management Team should be one of 'nervous self belief'. It is then crucial that this process is followed with the sales teams and they to end up in a state of nervous self belief. Then whenever one succeeds, the Regional Manager, Sales Director, and Managing Director all contribute as appropriate to the celebration of that success.

Case 2: Management Team consolidation

The second example was not specifically a profit improvement program. The aim was to consolidate and train a young and inexperienced management team. The business was in heavy engineering, manufacturing steel-formed products. Over a period of two years, there had been substantial reduction in staff numbers, major change in strategic focus and change in ownership. The new management team was now in place and the aim was to develop more effective teamwork and strengthen individual manager skills in relation to the role they held in the team.

Developing a manager does not occur without developing the person. Management skills are not something we slip on as we walk on the job each morning. There is some element of professional conduct, but there is also a strong element of personal development. Imagine coping with the death of someone very close. Some days we do not want to get out of bed, but we must. After coming through the grieving period, it is common for people to say how they feel they have grown – they feel stronger and able to cope with more than before. I believe that this is a result of the struggle to cope with the challenge of a situation where some days one is not sure of getting through the day. Growth of coping skills and self-assurance is brought about by the struggle of winning over a challenge. It is this that I believe leads to the other idea that success in sport makes for better and stronger men and women. I apply the philosophy in manager development by first establishing a challenging goal for the team that will stretch their skills and application. This can of course only be done in conjunction with the managing director, who must understand the process and accept it, and be quietly firm and committed in the face of the inevitable cries that they are working hard already. Once the creative challenge is established, the team is then offered coaching support and guidance in how to meet the challenge. For the great majority, it is an invigorating experience, but there are the occasional few for whom it is not.

The process begins with the business growth spreadsheet. This is a battle for such a team. The stretch required, the pressure of making something happen that otherwise will not, and the implicit questioning of their skills all result in creating an emotional and fractured environment. The process follows a quite predictable path from resistance, to grudging acceptance that more is possible, to passive resistance and an unaware failure to act, to a slow understanding of what it really takes to add momentum to a business. As these attitudes and emotions are settled, the team is also addressing its collective and individual skills and the need for an integrated effort if the result is really to be achieved. Teamwork is those actions by each person that will ensure the best possible result for the team – for a management team, that is the best possible operating profit. For each team member achieving the best possible result means doing all they can do to enhance operating profit and doing nothing that will undermine or detract from the efforts of any other team member. This in itself takes some time and discussion before it is understood and acted upon.

Slowly, steadily the team emerges into a state of nervous or anxious self-belief. A combination of understanding, seeing how it can be done and belief there are the skills in the team to do it. The spreadsheet that emerged is below.

Business Growth Plan for ..... Enginering business Years 2000/2001

Budget or best estimate		Projects and their effects				Projected after-effect of projects	
			Current year effects		Year 1 effects		
Profit profile	Opening £	£ Sales Projects	Sales	Costs	Sales	Costs	Current year £	Year 1 £
Revenue	£10,308,000	1 Achieve better prices	£150,000		£250,000			
		2 Improve prospecting and coverage	£450,000	£375,000	£650,000	£546,000		
		3					£10,683,000	£11,208,000
		4						
		Total sales change			£1,200,000			
		Direct costs change from sales projects		£375,000		£546,000		
		Direct cost projects						
Direct costs	£8,168,000	1 Reduce steel waste	-£45,000		-£25,000			
		2 Improve productivity by better planning	-£150,000		-£100,000			
		3 Improve business processes in plant	-£100,000		-£200,000		£8,248,000	£8,389,000
		4						
		Total direct cost changes	£		£			
			£335,000		£221,000			
Gross profit	£2,140,000						£2,435,000	£2,389,000
		Overhead projects						
Overheads	£1,599,000	1 Reduce freight loss	-£15,000		-£35,000			
		2 Allow for overhead escalation	£		£75,000			
		3	£		£		£1,584,000	£1,544,000
		4	£		£			
		Total overhead changes	-£15,000		-£40,000			
Operating profit	£541,000						£851,000	£1,275,000
% gross profit	%						%	%
% profit to sales	5%						8%	11.40%
£ increase in profit							**£310,000**	**£234,000**

Case 3: Improving retail profits

The final example is a straightforward project involving improving the profits in a small retail chain. The chain sold hardware, with four stores. It was run by a husband and wife team, the husband the managing director and operations director, the wife the administration and customer services manager. The chief point of interest is in the necessary expansion of the management team of the business and who should be included. Before the project, the 'management' was seen as the two owners, plus another person who looked after their small warehouse and was generally the purchasing manager. An important key to success in a retail chain is the skill and focus of the team leaders in each store. In the initial defining of this project, we agreed that the present management team became effectively the Board of Directors, and the new management team was to include the store team leaders. These people were not strictly managers, but they could and did have considerable influence on the focus and energy exhibited by the people in each of the stores.

The second crucial note in the spreadsheet is gaining understanding of the roles of each of the teams. It was agreed that the store teams would be accountable for the day-to-day feel, layout and energy in the store. These factors came to account in the percentage of people who came into the store and purchased something and came to account in the average invoice. Of the two, it was agreed that the average invoice was the most important. This was then to be increased by (1) reducing the level of discount offered to the trade customers who came into the stores and (2) by deliberately focusing on 'add on sales' with every sale. The head office or 'central team' as we agreed to call it, was responsible for the level of foot-traffic in the stores and for the overall range of product and product availability in the store. In short, the central team was expected to stock the store and provide foot-traffic and the store teams then had to ensure the store was presented so as to provide the best possible customer service and sales.

Business Growth Plan for ..... Retail hardware chain | **Years 2000/2001**

Budget or best estimate		Projects and their effects					Projected after-effect of projects	
Profit profile	Opening	£ Sales Projects	Current year effects		Year 1 effects		Current year £	Year 1 £
			Sales	Costs	Sales	Costs		
Revenue	£8,400,000	1 Reduce discounting	£100,000		£150,000		£8,800,000	£9,600,000
		2 Improve in-store selling	£150,000	£90,000	£250,000	£150,000		
		3 Introduce new range of product	£150,000	£90,000	£400,000	£240,000		
		4						
		Total sales change	£400,000		£800,000			
		Direct costs change from sales projects		£180,000		£390,000		
		Direct cost projects						
Direct costs	£5,796,000	1 Improve buying on five key lines		-£35,000		-£40,000	£5,891,000	£6,207,000
		2 Redce shrinkage from 2% to 1.4 and then 1%		-£50,000		-£34,000		
		3		£		£		
		4		£		£		
		Total direct cost changes		£95,000		£316,000		
Gross profit	£2,604,000						£2,909,000	£3,393,000
		Overhead projects						
Overheads	£1,824,000	1 Improve goods handling, reduce staff by 2		-£60,000		£	£3,735,000	£3,850,000
		2 Cost of new range		£100,000		£50,000		
		3 Overhead escalation		£		£90,000		
		4		£		£		
		Total overhead changes		£115,000		£140,000		
Operating profit	£780,000						£1,045,000	£1,389,000
% gross profit	31%						33%	35.30%
% profit to sales	9.30%						11.90%	14.50%
£ increase in profit							**£265,000**	**£609,000**

65

Conclusion on case studies

In each case the business growth spreadsheet was supported first by a simple, one or two page strategic outline. This focused on what the business did, who the customers were, and what service the business would provide for those customers. The second document was an annual budget giving the detail of the costs and revenues. The business growth spreadsheet then enabled the key management team to firstly focus on achieving the budget and then on the extra creative and emotional effort to add momentum to the business.

Review of these examples will show the nature of the projects under different circumstances and how the spreadsheet summarises the detail and provides a simple yet effective reporting framework for the team.

References

1. Willmot, Peter, Total Quality with Teeth, TQM Magazine, Vol: 6, Issue: 4, 1994, pages 48-50

2. Bryan, Eugene L., Ongoing Change Management. Executive Excellence, Vol: 11, Issue: 4, April 1994, pages: 11-12

3. Rutledge, John, Just Do It, Forbes, Vol: 15, Issue: 4 , February 14 1994, page 142

4. Yandrick, Rudy M., Organizational Addiction, HR Magazine, Vol: 39 Issue: 12, December 1994, pages 92-95

5. Kanellos, Michael, Active management, Key to Success for Retailers. Computer Resellers News. Issue : 599, October 10 1994, pages 133-136

6. Kepner-Tregoe Consultancy, Surveys Reveal some Executives Ignore the Human Side of their Organizations. Canadian Manager. Vol: 19, Issue: 4 December 1994, page 20

7. Neisley, Joe, Learning the Ultimate Lesson in Partnering, Computer News, February 29 1994, page 108

8. Harrell, Wilson I, Slaying Giants, Success. Vol: 41, Issue: 8, October 1994, page 106

9. Harrison, D. Brian & Conn, Henry P., Mobilising Abilities through Teamwork, Canadian Business Review. Vol: 21, Issue: 3, Autumn 1994, pages 20-22

10. Mullin, Rick, Dictates for the Top, Suggestion from the Floor. Chemical Week, Vol: 155, Issue: 10, September 21, 1994, pages 33-36

11. Anonymous. Team Yakka is Paying Nicely for Company and Workers, Work and People, Vol: 15, Issue: 1, July 1994 pages 6-7

12. Anonymous. Japan to the Rescue, German Brief, Vol: 6, Issue: 18, May 6 1994, pages 4-5

13. Owen, Jean V. & Epram, Eugene E., Shop Floor '94: The Power

of Partnerships, Manufacturing Engineering , Vol: 112, Issue: 4, April 1994, pages 33-42

14. Cosco, Joseph, Service with a Smile, Journal of Business Strategy, Vol: 15, Issue: 2 March/April 1994, pages 58-60

15. Markowich, M. Michael, Does Money Motivate? Compensation and Benefits Review, Vol: 25, Issue: 1, January/February 1994, pages 69-72

16. Markowich, M. Michael, Is your Company's Revenue Greater than it's Expenses? HR Focus.Vol: 71, Issue:1 January 1994, pages 4-6

17. Tracey, John A., Profit Dynamics, Dow Jones-Irwin, Homewood, Illinois 60430, 1989

18. Welsh, Glenn A., Budgeting: Profit Planning and Control, Englewood Cliffs, NJ, Prentice-Hall, 1988, 4th edition

19. Dick-Larkam, Richard, Profit Improvement Techniques: an Action Programme for Management. Epping, Essex, Gower Press, 1973

20. Lines, James, Profit Improvement: a comprehensive approach to improving managerial effectiveness, London, Business Books, 1973

21. Senju, Shizno, Profitability analysis: Japanese Approach, Tokyo, Asian Productivity Organisation, 1989

Improve unit costs

Set clear goals that produce the energy of challenge

Develop clear goals for all production departments

There are two major sources of such goals. The first is immediate profit improvement. Improvements in production downtime, waste control, overheads, power and productivity all lead to immediate increases in profit. The second is technological improvement. The development of a new process or product, or the refinement of an existing process or product, is determined by the direction in which the organisation wants to go.

To derive particular goals for your particular operation, you need to talk to your supervisors and departmental heads, pointing out the opportunities and asking them to reflect on what improvements could be made. In addition, there must be clear standards of performance for each department. For example, the polishing department must have clear standards relating to productivity, quality control and waste control. Similarly, the assembly department must have clear standards for its assembly operation. These standards then need to be broken down for each of the sections of a particular department. The staff in those sections need to be told what is expected of them with respect to those standards.

It is essential that these standards and goals are made relevant to people's behaviour within the workplace. There is no point in giving them standards and goals as they might be understood by the production manager or, even worse, the general manager. Break the standards and goals down so that they become very specific and staff can immediately see the impact of their behaviour on those standards and goals. Review standards of performance against your goals regularly. Provide people with qualified information relating to those goals. If a goal relates to a machine's through-put, give the operator data about how much through-put there was last week, last month or whatever the appropriate time scale is. Preferably review through-put on a weekly basis; this gives people the opportunity to respond immediately if it decreases. Setting up this structure of goals and standards takes time and care. It is not something that can be rushed.

Have a clear plan for improving the production unit

If you are going to adopt an assembly line operation, full automation is the key and all development plans should be concentrated on automation. It is beyond the resources of most companies to automate a whole assembly line immediately, so it should be prioritised. The plan should be in place and you should make it happen. If it is to be a jobbing shop, then work hard at getting those jobbing skills handed to peak performance. Work hard on improving every facet of the operation. It is always possible to tighten current operations and thus improve productivity.

However, long-term developmental goals will often come into conflict with short-term cost-saving goals. The relationship between these goals needs to be properly understood. Realising your vision for the organisation may well involve significant expenditure. At any point there may be a drive to reduce or contain expenditure. Your job as manager is to establish the balance between forward investment and immediate cost savings.

Instill a bottom-up attitude towards improvements

When you are seeking profit improvements through immediate expense control, waste reduction or productivity improvement, you should talk to people as low down the organisation as you possibly can about the details of what is happening in their section or department. Do not imagine that you can sit in your office as the production manager and fully grasp the details of a particular process and how it can be improved. Go and ask the people involved. The implementation of such concepts as work improvement, quality circles and similar techniques will involve the operators themselves in the drive for improved performance. The key, of course, is the attitude of senior management and the attitude that they pass on to their staff.

Production goals must include response to customers

Examine the following areas:

- the length of time a telephone rings before being answered
- the number of times a customer fails to get everything on an order
- the number of customer complaints
- the number of sales lost through out-of-stocks
- production lead time.

Work with your staff to establish clear standards of performance with respect to the customer. Then quietly lead them to live by these standards.

Ask your staff how goals can be achieved

Manage by walking around. But, when walking around, you should have a clear idea of what you expect of your people. You should be conscious of the attitudes you require, and the degree of responsiveness you want to customers and quality. When you perceive a problem, approach people quietly and ask how things can be improved and what they would do. Have your own ideas in mind, but do not necessarily impose these on your staff first. Then you should hold meetings with your supervisors and departmental heads, asking how things could be improved. The key to managing such meetings is to avoid letting them degenerate into complaint sessions. Focus people on things that they are responsible for and can control. Ask how it can be done. Live out your philosophy – it's difficult but possible. The key is the extent to which you are prepared to stretch and set goals beyond your immediate comfort zone. And you must also encourage your staff to set goals for themselves beyond their comfort zone. When they achieve such goals, of course, it is a very satisfying and worthwhile event.

Understand the conflict between goals

At times, goals may be in conflict. Your department heads and senior supervisors need to understand this. The extent to which they have this insight will determine their management potential. Not all will understand as well as you might like. This conflict will become evident as you try to take your production unit towards the vision you have for it, while simultaneously keeping expenses under tight control. The management of such conflict demands creativity, insight, experience, good judgment, understanding, patience and lots of energy.

Build profit consciousness

Make every effort to improve margins

There are two key factors in improving margins:

• Gain the commitment of the people.
• Give them guidance on where they should commit their energy.

We will consider gaining the commitment of people in later sections. For now, I wish to examine guiding and directing people in terms of where they should place their energy for the improvement of manufacturing margins. The scheme below will guide thinking about margins, leading to practical and immediate goal-setting and increased effort in order to improve those margins. Once you have decided where margins can be improved, it is then important to establish specific, detailed goals.

For instance, given a goal of '*Improve purchasing methods, replace suppliers*', how could purchasing methods be improved?

• Are better lead times possible?

- Could you give suppliers greater warning of off-take requirements?

- Is it possible to establish simple visual systems that give an earlier indication of out-of-stocks and stock shortages?

- Is it possible to replace some suppliers with more effective suppliers and to reduce the prices?

- Is it possible to get a better deal out of existing suppliers?

- When was the last time suppliers of key raw materials were researched to the point where you were confident that you had the best deal that could be obtained?

Similar questions should be asked for all the other ways of improving margins. Providing this ongoing guidance for the organisation is a critical role for the production manager.

Improving manufacturing margins

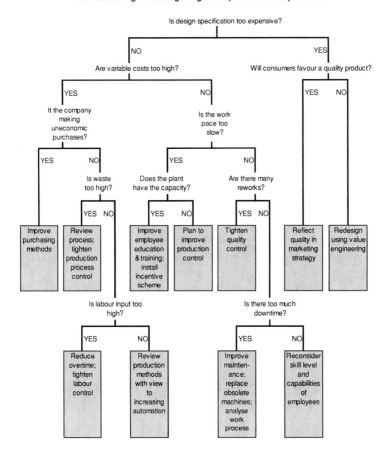

Balance immediate profits against medium- and long-term profits

It is always possible to reduce costs. And cost reductions are always beneficial in that they result in an immediate improvement in profitability. However, cost reductions can also have their disadvantages. For instance, they can engender a mean attitude among staff. This can in itself result in a tone being conveyed to clients and suppliers that makes them uncomfortable in dealing with the company. While this may not have an immediate effect, it may have a longer-term impact on the profitability of the company. Cost reductions can also be taken too far. For instance, service levels may be reduced, and while this may result in immediate cost savings, the long-term effect may be slowing-down or even a loss of sales. Cost reductions may also restrict product development, and they may discourage the thinking that leads to product innovation. This too could have disastrous long-term consequences for the company. The production manager must balance the requirements of immediate profits against the necessary commitment of resources for activities such as service that may appear expensive in the short term but in the long term provide the stability of customer reassurance. It is essential to balance short-term cost reductions against activities such as product development and research that will bring longer-term profits and growth to the company.

Encourage practical, daily thrift and expense control as the norm

Encourage staff to think about the little, everyday savings that can be made. A manufacturing plant in New Zealand employed a large number of Polynesian workers. The staff had to handle big, extremely expensive moulds. Unfortunately these were frequently mishandled, resulting in very high replacement and repair costs. The company talked to the staff and told them how expensive they were, but somehow the message did not seem to be absorbed. In the end, the company printed messages on the moulds such as: 'This is the same amount of money as your airfare back to Fiji or Rarotonga' or 'This mould is of the same value as your village on your island'. Putting the expense in these terms, terms that people understood resulted in an immediate reduction in mishandling. Don't merely berate people; get the message across to them in terms that they can understand.

Opportunities for simple expense control relate to power, waste, the use and respect of tools, the use of trucks and other vehicles, toll calls, and exercising reasonable self-discipline with respect to time-keeping and productivity. All these items need to be controlled. But, in addition to management control, the production manager and supervisors need to encourage a positive attitude and exhibit this attitude themselves at all times. Many of the items can only be controlled by management up to a point, and for savings beyond that the people themselves need to exercise the discipline. The production manager who successfully instills this self-disciplined approach among his or her staff will always have a cost-effective plant.

Ensure that every employee helps the company stay profitable

A business is in business to make a profit. Every person in the company carries out his or her job in order to contribute to this. Promote this simple perspective. State it quietly – do not berate people with it, or attack them with it, or sneer at them about it, or be cynical with them about it – but do not allow them to forget it. Encourage profitability as the measure of success. In particular, encourage a long-term approach to the concept of profitability. The issue is not merely how much profit you made this month or even this year, but whether the company will have long-term stability and what its long-term profit trend will be. Get people to strive to contribute to the improvement of company profile and to measure their personal success in relation to the company's success. This is an essential leadership task. To realise this goal, you yourself must be committed to these things, believe them resolutely, and be able to state them with quiet, firm conviction.

Guide supervisors and staff in generating ideas to improve profits

There are two essential sorts of leadership: direct, interpersonal leadership (i.e. direct supervision) and conceptual or visionary leadership. An entrepreneur, managing director or general manager providing lots of focus and direction would perhaps be described as visionary. A production manager or manager, on the other hand, providing the same type of focus and direction, is more likely to be described as a direct leader, but his or her role is no less visionary. Even production supervisors who are providing the direction and focus for their team (that is, how the team can improve performance, productivity, cost control, waste control or quality) are providing visionary leadership. They are providing the team with the longer-term goal and the focus for that goal, and assisting the team to establish exactly what each will do in order to achieve that goal. This is an essential task management. In order to provide this leadership immediately, you need to implement two simple steps.

- **Step one: select a particular area that you think could be improved.** This could be waste control, power conservation, productivity, quality control, service, invoicing, routing of deliveries, routing of raw materials through the plant, storage of raw materials, storage of waste, storage of finished product or handling and storage of work in progress – whatever it might be, select one.

- **Step two: ask your people: 'How do you think we could improve in this particular area?'** Generate ideas, select some of the sensible ones, have them researched a little, meet again to reassess them and their value, effectiveness and ease of implementation, then implement two or three of them. Once those ideas have been implemented and shown to be successful, be sure to provide interpersonal leadership by congratulating and if possible rewarding the staff involved.

Then get the team back together again and review more ideas that can be implemented with respect to the previous area, or select a new area and repeat the whole process.

Provide the management standard by seeking one such improvement every month.

Create profit-improvement strategies for your production unit

Follow these simple steps:

- **Step one:** select an area for improvement.
- **Step two:** generate ideas, choose the best one, then do it.

In business you have only two things going for you: your energy and your judgment. Selecting the area to focus on in order to improve profitability and balance long-term and short-term profit gains is a matter of judgment. Talk about it with your manager, with the chairman of the board, with the shop-floor supervisor, with the operators on the factory floor, with the managing director, with fellow production managers from other units, and with other production managers from different companies, and go on training courses where you might get some new ideas. But at the end of the day, having done all that talking and thinking, and collected all the opinions and ideas, it is your judgment that goes on the line. But judge you must, for without judging first you will never act. Once you have exercised your judgment, then you must apply your energy and your enthusiasm to sell your judgment to the people directly involved and to involve them in the brainstorming process and the application of their creative powers to the area you have chosen in order to come up with ideas for improvements. Judgment and energy – you must use both constantly and effectively.

Create profit-improvement strategies for each product

Follow these simple steps:

- **Step one:** select a product or product group for improvement.
- **Step two:** generate ideas, choose the best one, then do it.

Apply the margin-improvement scheme in the section, making every effort to improve margins to each product and product group. Select the product group that has the best potential for improvement – for example, where components could be made more cheaply, or the purchase of a piece of equipment could save costs, or the volume is such that small improvements in margin can have a major effect on profitability. Apply sound judgment to the selection of the products or product groups that are to be given priority.

Once you have selected the products or product groups, research them carefully, then involve the appropriate people in a brainstorming process to find means of improving the margins. In carrying out this task, you are reinforcing margin improvement and the need for the organisation to better itself as a key part of your philosophy and culture. By you doing this constantly, you get a clear message across to your people, so that slowly but surely this striving for improvement will become the norm.

Stress the importance of serving the customer

Products, operations, and factories do not operate within a vacuum, although sometimes one might think so. It is trite to say 'The customer is king', but this idea has somehow to be conveyed to your staff. Often they will agree that the customer is important, then act in ways quite opposed to this principle. It is your job to encourage your people to act as if the customer is important. Profits are not merely a consequence of producing well. A company may be able to produce well, but if nobody wants its product, it will still not be profitable. Raise customer awareness. Think of ten things you could do to improve customer awareness. Select five, and do them. Then think of ten more, select five, and do them.

Ensure an ongoing work improvement program

Ask staff how standards of performance could be improved

The foreman in the packing and despatch department of a pharmaceutical company was trying to improve the productivity of his three packing teams. The teams consisted of a total of 17 women. He had frequently timed their operations, he had supervised the department for 12 years and knew every aspect of it in considerable detail, and he had recently rearranged the work benches, schedule and work pattern in an attempt to raise productivity. By and large this

79

had failed. He attended a range of lectures on supervision and motivation, and was impressed with the idea of using team performance standard setting to improve productivity.

So he approached his employees and put it to them. To his dismay, the standard of performance that they came up with was in fact lower than what they had been achieving before. This left him with a major problem.

It is not a matter of just asking your team what they can do. The asking has to be done with integrity. The foreman above had made repeated attempts to enforce the standard of performance he thought was necessary. When he finally approached his team and asked them, they knew full well it was simply another manipulative act in an attempt to raise the standard of performance. And the team proceeded to mete out appropriate justice to this inept supervisory act. It is essential that people are approached openly and sincerely. They may be cynical and sceptical, and often they will have good reason to be so. The process of engaging them in the establishment of their own production standards, while at the same time educating them on the realities of what production standards the company needs in order to stay effectively and competitively in business, must be based on this openness and sincerity and, above all, initially, on patience.

A key objective for all production managers should be to involve all their staff in establishing standards of performance for quality and productivity. Do this effectively, and your plant will certainly succeed.

Constantly seek opportunities for further improvement

Progressive, bottom-up productivity improvement should be a major process established within all production units. This process is based first and foremost on the determination to improve. The first task, then, is to sell the philosophy and values consistent with work improvement to the staff. This is probably the most difficult task, and it is a problem, or a project, discussed throughout this book. To do this successfully, you, as leader, must make sure that your own attitudes and behaviour are completely consistent with this philosophy. Opportunities for improvement could relate to the following areas.

- **In the factory:** dirty, difficult and tiring jobs, lengthy or tedious jobs, repetitive work, unsafe operations or actions, the use and tidiness of factory floor space, the internal transport of materials, the manning of machines and plant, or the issue of supplies and tools.

- **In the office:** the design of forms (shape, size and colour), the design and maintenance of records, the appropriate use of new technology and computing, filing letters, records and documents, the use of office space and desk arrangements, the establishment of passageways, cutting red tape and simplifying procedures, eliminating faulty clerical work, or scheduling work.

- **In the store:** the layout of displays of merchandise, fixing counter lines and passageways, the movement of merchandise in and out of the storeroom, cutting materials and subdividing stock items, writing out dockets or crediting returns, using cash registers or tube carriers, or counting stock and keeping records.

When not busy, the supervisors, under your guidance, should make a survey of their sections to determine which methods can be improved, remembering always that there is more than one way to do a job. Sell the concept of bottom-up improvement to your people, encourage each of them to become involved in improving what they do in their job, then watch the effect the improvements have on your budget.

Coach key staff in the key steps of work improvement

There are six essential steps in work improvement.

- ✓ **Step 1:** Select the job that you are going to improve. It should make work safer or easier, reduce excessive movement, or eliminate bottlenecks.

- ✓ **Step 2:** Keep records. Enlist the co-operation of the operator, study the work being done, analyse the present method, and then note any difficulties or opportunities for improvement.

✓ **Step 3:** Examine what happens now.

- What is achieved? Is it necessary? Why?
- Where is it done? Why there? What other place would be better?
- When is it done? Why then? What other time would be better?
- Who does it? Why that person? What other person would be better?
- How is it done? Why in that way? What other way would be better?

Note all the ideas. Consider, in particular, safety, quality, design, layout, equipment and materials.

✓ **Step 4:** Review all the ideas in your analysis above. Eliminate, simplify, combine and rearrange. Consult the people who are to be affected, and chart a new method. This step is the key creative step, the brainstorming step where you generate ideas about how things could be done differently and then evaluate those ideas in terms of practicality. Finally, a key question in step four: **could the whole job itself in fact be eliminated?**

✓ **Step 5:** Once you have established a new method, <u>install it</u>. Train the staff in its use.

✓ **Step 6:** Maintain the new method by frequent checks and carefully watching results.

Apply the rules for fatigue reduction and placement of personnel

Reduce fatiguing movements that waste energy:

1. Transfer all heavy lifting to mechanical devices.
2. Use momentum rather than force.
3. Continuous curved motions are easier and less tiring than motions involving sharp changes in direction.

4. Use that part of the body most competent to perform the operation.
5. Use the body to the best mechanical advantage so that work is performed at the right height and position.
6. Eliminate working conditions that contribute to fatigue.
7. On heavy jobs it is better to have many short rest periods than a few long rest periods.
8. On monotonous jobs provide occasional breaks.

Utilise personnel to the best advantage:

- Let each operative specialise in a particular activity.
- Fit the individual to the job specifications.
- Use the higher-paid workers on the more complicated tasks requiring greater skill and experience.

Get good operators to coach other staff

What attitudes within the plant result from using good operators to train other operators? The chief danger is the establishment of rivalry between operators if one operator is to train another. Therefore, the selection of people to do the training of others needs to be done with some caution; you must ensure that the people selected to do the training have credibility and the respect of the other operators. This can be quickly checked merely by talking to some of the staff likely to be trained.

The second issue to be aware of is that the people doing the training may tend to feel that they have some power or authority that you have not intended to give them. They may begin to issue orders or develop an inflated view of their own activities within the plant. This also has to be managed with due sensitivity and care. The overall benefit of adopting this process is that operators within the plant will become accustomed to teaching one another about what they are good at. This will lead to an overall climate of growth, helpfulness, and improved productivity – some of the key goals of any production manager.

Encourage the creative efforts of your key staff

When supervisors or senior operators approach you with a problem in the plant, do not immediately offer a solution, even though you will often be able to do so. Instead, ask, 'What would you do?' Then follow this with, 'Well, that's one option. What else would you do?' Then again, 'What else could you do?' Once they have generated three or four ideas, perhaps including an idea or two of yours, assess all the options, select one, approve it, then reinforce them by saying, 'There, you didn't need me to solve that problem after all.' On a more formal basis, within departments or sections of your production unit, encourage regular brainstorming sessions concentrating on problems to be overcome, particular aspects of the work to be improved, or how quality or productivity can be raised. If there is a quality circle programme, this will clearly be part of it. But even where there is no formal quality circle programme, or something similar, such activities are always beneficial and should be encouraged. The essential ingredient in the success of such work groups is to ensure that they stay focused on the practical things that they can themselves control and implement. There is no point in such groups working out how to improve marketing if they have no influence on marketing and no particular expertise in that area. People need to be told to focus on their expertise – that is, on their own job and their own area of control.

Have a work-improvement target or project every month

It does not matter if the target is large or small. Aim for one practical improvement to be achieved in your plant every month, even if it is only a saving of £10. The important thing is to establish the philosophy, attitudes and behaviour consistent with ongoing productivity improvement. Wherever practical, ensure that your supervisors have improvement targets, but do not necessarily set the targets yourself. Your job is to see it happen, not necessarily to do it. It is the appropriate philosophy and behaviour that you should seek first and foremost. Invest in the creative resource of your people, and focus it by encouraging them to concentrate on things they can control and improve.

Ensure clear labour standards

Establish labour standards

A labour standard is the work in minutes required to complete an element of an operational product under ordinary operating conditions. Labour standards are hierarchical – that is, each element or basic task is a standard; these add up to give the labour standard for each operation; and these add up to give the labour standard for the product.

There are a number of ways of establishing labour standards.

- The first is time study – that is, observing the current level of performance and adopting this as the standard.

- The second is predetermining time standards. Use data already established for basic body movements, such as the movement of hands. (Data are available from Methods Time Measurement Association, 16/01 Broadway, Fairlawn, NJ, 07410, USA.) The time for basic body movements can be assessed from the available data.

- The third way of establishing labour standards is by work sampling – random sampling of the output from workers, departments or machines to find out the number of units produced in a given time period.

Once the labour standard has been established, work improvement techniques should be applied to progressively improve it. The techniques for achieving this method improvement should involve all those that have been discussed elsewhere in this book. Above all, you must involve the staff who have to do the operations. They are the ones who know best the practical issues involved.

Discuss with staff the purpose and use of labour standards

Labour standards and their establishment can be threatening. However, labour standards are essential if accurate pricing of the product is to be achieved. They also provide a guide to productivity within the plant. These factors need to be explained to the staff; they need to understand the underlying rationale and philosophy. Staff should not be dominated by labour standards; they should be able to effectively achieve them if they work consistently at a steady pace. No plant should expect its operatives to run all the time.

It is essential that the philosophy of labour standards is sold to the production staff. This is the task of the production manager. This should be followed with creative brainstorming sessions to improve on these standards on a regular basis. And improving on these standards can be one of the regular monthly goals for method improvement. Labour standards can be used in a number of ways, one of the most important of which is the establishment of accurate pricing. They are also useful in calculating the number of operatives required per week or the labour performance of a department. Major variances should then be analysed. It is important that labour standards are, in fact, realistic. You should be aware, when using some of the techniques, such as predetermined time standards, that they often do not take account of some of the practical limitations of the situation, the particular product, or the flow of work. Labour standards should always be adjusted so that they are seen as an effective and sensible guide to performance arid productivity.

Provide staff with regular feedback on their performance

It is essential that staff are provided with regular weekly or monthly information on their performance in terms that they can understand and relate immediately to their behaviour on the job. This information should usefully relate to the labour standards that they know and understand and accept. This information can be provided via the supervisor, or via the regular meeting, or via the notice board, reinforced by word of mouth. It is often useful to have a competitive element, and this can be managed by the supervisor drawing attention to those who succeed – that is, those who meet the standard or exceed the standard – and politely refraining from commenting on those who fail to meet the suitable standard. It is important not to chastise those who do not meet the standard, unless this is an ongoing problem, in which case the supervisor should take the individual aside and have a private discussion with him or her about it. The individual should not be disciplined in public for failing to meet the standard.

Accept current labour standards and then seek to improve on them

If you are implementing labour standards for the first time, or if the labour standards are not widely or readily accepted as standards, then you need to begin with caution. The first step should be to discuss and have accepted the principle of labour standards – how they can be used, their importance, and how they should be arrived at. As a starting point in tightening labour standards, it is best to accept the current methods and standard of work and adopt a creative and brainstorming approach aimed at improving on those standards.

Develop a competitive but co-operative climate

Effective management often involves finding the right balance between competing principles. Within any effective organisation there must be co-operation, but there must also be competition.

The art is to blend competition into a co-operative ethic, so that competition drives the organisation towards increasingly better performance without blunting the professional co-operation necessary for any organisation to effectively serve its customers. To achieve this blend, the manager must understand the nature of the issue and then do two fundamental things. First, the reporting system and information flow should emphasise teams, and the competitive performance of those teams in improving output, expense control, customer satisfaction, service, reduction in waste, or whatever other variable is appropriate. This information system can be reinforced by the occasional use of rewards for the winner of a particular competition. For example, the team that produces the highest output of a certain product over a given period of time may be awarded an extra holiday or a video or a trip to Paris. In this way, competition is created, fostered and reinforced. The second thing the manager must do – and this is critical – is manage team ethics so that the competition engendered by the formal information system does not flow across into interpersonal rivalry, politics, or destructive information hoarding.

To manage the tension between conflict and co-operation, the manager must separate the two. Conflict and competition are engendered by formal information processes emphasising the teams and the performance of those teams. Co-operation is then managed by ensuring tight control of the ethics of the teams and the interaction between them – that is, the manager manages tightly how each person within the unit treats the others. It is essential that the manager personally acts out this philosophy. It is important that people do not run down a team competing with theirs, and that they always treat opposing teams with due respect. They must always act in a professional, co-operative manner to ensure that the organisation as a whole is not disadvantaged by competition between teams. Competition should be restricted to the formal information system; co-operation should always be evident in people's behaviour.

Improve purchasing

Understand that suppliers are as essential as customers

Both suppliers and customers are essential for the success of the company, and both should be treated with respect. Begin by working harder at providing more accurate forecasts earlier.

Suppliers have their own plans and lead times. Better planning will help avoid missing deadlines.

As part of the process of involving suppliers in your business, demand some open accounting. Offer commitment in exchange for knowledge of profit levels, gross margins and production practices. Involve your staff with the appropriate staff of the supplier. In this way, supervisor can contact supervisor to avoid a problem becoming a major production delay. Make a commitment to the supplier, but in return, expect openness, sensible profit levels, and a willingness to understand and assist your business. In return for contributing to your success, they will gain long-term commitment from you. Involve your suppliers in your business, and involve yourself in theirs. Create a win-win situation. Do not treat your suppliers as people outside your business. Be loyal to them, but seek performance in return. Give your suppliers the best possible opportunities to perform on your behalf. Bring them in and treat them as you might treat an employee – discipline them, praise them, and manage them as you would manage any other employee. But if, at the end of the day, they still do not perform, then you may well have to attend to them as you would attend to any other non-performing employee. With reluctance, but nonetheless with careful planning, precision and whilst taking best care of your own business, you must replace them.

Check all suppliers' prices and terms every year

Negotiate prices with directness and vigour. Check every price with at least two other suppliers and maintain this market overview on a regular basis. New suppliers come and go, technologies change, suppliers that were potentially unprofitable some time ago may now be profitable. In addition, your existing suppliers, which may have been the most competitive five years ago, may now have out-of-date plant and equipment. They may also be reluctant to upgrade their plant and equipment and so make their prices competitive in the modern market. These factors need to be examined. At the same time, your decisions about suppliers should not be based only on price. Price is critical, but it is not necessarily the sole factor. Your people know the staff of your existing suppliers; your existing suppliers know and understand your business, because you have trained them in that. You must take these factors into account when you are determining whether or not to change suppliers.

Establish a purchasing-control report. Every item purchased should be listed with the previous and latest price. Treat your purchasing department as another department with a contribution to make to profits – by buying at prices lower than last year's, wherever possible, or, at the very least, at prices less than the budgeted increases. In this way, the purchasing department can be financially accountable in terms of contributing to the profits of the organisation. Be sure to obtain references for all new suppliers. Treat potential suppliers as you would treat potential employees. They are just as important to you. Once suppliers are supplying you a product or component or service, manage them thoroughly to achieve what you want from them.

Where possible, establish simple, visual inventory-control systems

A self-assembly kitchen manufacturer attempted to control stocks of the panels and components that made up the kitchens with a relatively complex, though supposedly accurate, card system.

The system was never accurate. And the people who needed to know, never seemed to know how much stock they had, where it was, or how much was required. The system was reorganised.

There were approximately 800 components. Each was put in its own compartment, and a simple visual recording system was installed. Reordering was then very simple. Staff merely had to walk down the aisles between the racks containing the material and quickly observe what needed to be ordered and in what quantity.

Aim for simple, tightly controlled, practical organisation. Be sure that those who need information can obtain it readily and quickly, preferably without having to refer to computer print-outs or card files. This is not always possible. But where it is not, ensure that sensible and properly organised summary information is available so that people can refer to it quickly and secure the data they need.

Set policy guidelines on safety stocks and reorder points

Let us assume that a particular item is used at an average rate of 50 per week and it takes two weeks to receive an order from the supplier. At what level of inventory should an order be placed? The answer is 100 units (50 x 2) – that is, when the inventory falls to 100 units, an order should be placed. Now, let us assume that the conditions are as above except that, once every four weeks on average, either demand is greater than expected or deliveries are slowed so that an out-of-stock results in a loss of two sales. Further, let us assume that the profit from a sale is £5 and annual carrying costs amount to £30 per unit. Should a safety stock of two units be maintained? Over a year, 24 sales (2 X 12) or £120 in added profit will be lost. Since it only costs £30 per unit to maintain the safety stock (£60 total per year), profits exceed costs, so the safety stock should be maintained. By maintaining a two-unit safety stock, the total profit will be increased by £60. A study of sales records combined with your knowledge of the business will provide the data needed to calculate safety stocks. Maintaining the proper level of safety stocks can help you increase profits.

Carefully monitor inventory to ensure that it matches demand

Be ruthless in your regular reassessment of non-moving inventory and non-moving finished products or work in progress. It is all too easy to accumulate this or that component or inventory for lines that are no longer being produced or that have not been produced for many months but may be reintroduced soon. During stock-takes, it is also tempting to include such inventory in the stock count. Be ruthless, but be realistic. Product demand changes. Products, or components of products, that were fast moving last year may not be the fast movers now. Your stock levels may well reflect last year's sales volume and not current sales volume. When this occurs, you will have to stock up on the items that are moving most rapidly now; this will occur naturally and as a result you will become significantly overstocked with inventory. The main reason for this is that you have excessive inventory for products that are no longer moving at the rate they were previously. Therefore, you will have to find some way of managing those stocks down quickly and converting the capital represented by those stocks into more useful materials, or materials that are likely to move more quickly. This inventory-profile monitoring process should occur on a regular basis – at least half-yearly and preferably quarterly.

Monitor inventory regularly

Aim to control the following parameters with respect to inventory.

- **The overall inventory level** – you should have a policy guideline for the total inventory allowable for the organisation as a whole.

- **The inventory profile** – that is the mix of components and materials in relation to the current sales mix. You may need to have policy guidelines for every inventory item, this level being subject to review every quarter.

- **Inventory turn** – clearly this will be related to the inventory profile, and should be as high as practicable in relation to the lead time and convenient order quantities. The cost of inventory – that is, the total amount of capital that is nominated as inventory – again relates to the overall inventory level.

- **The forecasting of future sales** by the organisation is the key to effective inventory control and effective production management. Where a wide range of products is produced and forecasting is weak, high inventories are inevitable. Do not allow this to happen to your organisation. Otherwise, your return on capital will be lower than it needs to be.

Monitor lost sales due to out-of-stocks

Salespeople will want stocks to be as high as possible, so that customers are always served with what they want. Good business practice is to have the stock levels as low as possible and to minimise the amount of capital tied up in stock and inventory. This will typically reduce overdraft costs. A balance must always be struck between these two. Seek to assess the sales lost through out-of-stocks. Seek to quantify sales gains made by carrying more stock. Do not merely accept opinion. Research the problem. Then establish policy in relation to safety stock based on the increased profits that will accrue with increased investment of capital in the stock.

Reduce waste

Encourage waste reduction by every employee

Waste reduction should be constantly encouraged and exhibited by you and all your senior managers and supervisors as they move around the plant. It should also be encouraged through training courses, meetings and regular talks. It should be a topic that is regularly discussed in quality circles or similar discussion groups within the plant. There should be a sound understanding by all operatives in the plant of the impact of waste on the profitability of the company. At the same time, you should emphasise that, by controlling the waste they generate, employees are contributing to the success of the organisation.

Control waste

Think out the key strategies for controlling waste in your organisation.

- First, control the labour waste. Have tight labour standards and encourage supervisors to meet those standards. Monitor and control overtime.

- Second, control the effective use of raw materials; use jigs and carefully controlled cutting patterns.

- Identify all areas of high re-work; hold brainstorming meetings with key operatives and supervisors to generate ideas for reducing or even eliminating the re-works.

- Implement training programmes to increase skills and, in particular, improve attitudes.

- Monitor all faults found through inspection. Analyse the faults regularly to identify the major causes of rejection, then again hold brainstorming meetings with key operatives and supervisors in order to correct those faults and reduce the level of rejections. Improve the utilisation of materials, reduce re-works, and reduce rejections – make these part of your regular monthly performance-improvement goals.

- Examine carefully the handling of all raw materials coming into the plant. Be sure that they are handled in such a way that the material is not damaged. Again, where that is occurring, hold meetings with key supervisors and operatives to gather ideas on how the situation can be improved.

One organisation manufacturing steel bolts and nuts was losing 3 percent of its steel rod stock during forklift handling on arrival at the plant. Brainstorming with the operatives and supervisors reduced this to under 0.5 percent when they realised the significance of those bent rods at the bottom of the pile.

Control all aspects of waste, from labour, power and administration to raw materials and components. Excess waste is one of the major causes of profit erosion within production units.

Improve plant efficiency

Aim to systematically reduce component costs

As part of your ongoing performance-improvement and cost-saving drive, create a materials matrix. This consists of a list of all the components in the product, then the current material that the components are constructed from, followed by a range of alternative materials, including the lowest cost and the current cost. Be creative when generating the list of alternative materials – for instance, write down plastic or wood or bitumen, even if the material is not quite appropriate. Be conscious of the requirements of effective brainstorming. Don't be afraid to put the ideas down; you can never be sure where an idea that initially appears silly may lead. It is essential to think beyond traditional materials, using lateral thinking and brainstorming techniques. Set goals that force you to think widely. For example, how cheaply can the product be designed, regardless of quality or practicability? Creativity leads to practical profit-improvement ideas.

Minimise the movement of materials

Wherever possible, seek a direct flow of materials through the plant. Related production processes should be arranged to provide for this. Thus, in a wood-panel operation, the edgebander should follow the router. Mechanical material-handling devices should be designed and located, and material storage locations should be selected, so that human effort expended through bending, reaching, lifting, and walking is minimised.

Heavy or bulky materials should be moved the shortest distance through locating processes that use them near receiving and shipping areas. And the number of times each material is moved should be minimised. Overriding this, however, the system's flexibility should allow for unexpected situations, such as material-handling equipment breakdowns, changes in systems and technology, or future expansion of productive capacity.

Wherever possible, mobile equipment should carry full loads; empty and partial loads should be avoided. Where employees are involved in loading materials on or off a piece of equipment, the backlog of work behind them should be large enough for them to see there is adequate work flowing to them, but not so large as to be demotivating.

Staff should be expected to work at a steady, consistent pace; they should not be expected to work at an extremely fast pace all day. Supervisors should also understand that the pace people work at will vary according to the time of the day.

Where possible, the pace of work should be understood by employees, and there should be specific goals relating the amount of work carried out to a particular time scale. For instance, the amount of work put through an edge bander each day could be assessed and fed back to the operators working the machine.

Understand that a good flow of work is the key to productivity

There should be a smoothness in the flow of materials, from raw material to finished product. Avoid restrictions in the flow, sharp changes in the nature of the flow, and significant disruptions. When problems occur, use them as an opportunity to involve your operators in productivity- and profit-improvement problem-solving. The people most likely to be able to solve material-flow problems are those closest to them. They will have the most detailed knowledge of the nature of the problem, though they may not have the knowledge of material-handling technology that could provide a suitable solution. But they will certainly have some ideas on the effectiveness of any solution proposed. Talk to your supervisors about the smoothness of the flow through the plant; they will sense when it is right. And they will sense when it is not, though they will not always be conscious of this as a problem. Use the instinctive judgment of your people. Once an issue has been identified, focus the creative and problem-solving resources of your staff on the problem and resolve it.

Maintain quality

Have a clear, firm attitude towards quality

Adopt appropriate quality standards for your organisation. For example, if you run a high-quality and expensive restaurant serving sophisticated French cuisine, then the food, service and accommodation all need to be appropriate to your clientele and pricing levels. On the other hand, if you run a roadside diner for long-haul truck drivers your food may be steak, chips and eggs, and your accommodation basic, but the quality must still be there. The premises must be clean, tidy and well organised. Service needs to be with a smile and friendliness; your customers will be tired people who have driven a long way. The steak needs to be appropriately done, the chips and eggs should not be greasy, and the salad should not be limp. The quality should be high, regardless of the nature of the product.

Once you have determined the key quality factors that must pervade your operation, then you need to be sure that those quality factors are understood by your key staff, and that the reporting system focuses attention on them on a regular, at least monthly, basis.

A national training organisation had the quality problem of maintaining standards in the training room. It was a production operation like any other. To maintain attention on quality, every day, after every session, a minimum of three people were asked their opinions of the training during that session. And this was then distributed to all tutors nationally so that they could see the level of participant appreciation for every session they conducted every week. This certainly kept their attention on the quality of their efforts in the training room.

What are the key factors for your organisation? What are the key numbers you need people to concentrate on every week? Those numbers themselves will focus attention on the key quality issues, so that the individuals concerned can see what behaviour changes need to occur in order to bring those numbers back up to standard if they are below standard. Quality is critical. At all times your organisation should strive to achieve maximum value for money. Do this and do this well and you will always have a client.

Do not compromise the quality standard

It is often tempting to compromise the quality standard through expediency. For instance, if there is a large urgent job, you may allow the quality standard to slip in order to meet the deadline. If you are going to make that type of decision or are even considering it, you should first seek the customer's approval. If that is not possible, and you cannot get the customer's agreement, then do not compromise on the standard that is expected.

> A company manufacturing bathroom taps installed new automatic polishing equipment. The equipment produced a polished finish of lower quality than the old buffing wheels had achieved, and it did not significantly increase the production output. The supervisors were, to say the least, frustrated and dispirited by this arbitrary and unnecessary move by management, which effectively reduced the quality of the product they had previously been proud of. Their frustration was compounded when it was discovered that the owner of the buffing equipment franchise was closely related to the new managing director of the organisation. Two of the key supervisors resigned as a result.

Emphasise value for money in your production unit. Encourage your staff to focus on quality and their contribution to it. Customer satisfaction should be uppermost in the minds of all your people.

Regularly ask customers for their opinion on the quality

It is often quite threatening to ask customers what they think of your organisation and the products it produces. But there is no better way of assessing the security of your market. Customers can be asked in many ways – such as regular questionnaires utilising your sales force, focus groups where a selected group of customers visits your site for a meeting focusing on quality and company performance, or mass surveys by telephone or mail. Any one of these methods, or several of them, can be adapted and adopted to fit your needs. What is required is the will on your part to make knowledge of the customers' views sufficiently important to you and your organisation to ensure that it is surveyed on a regular basis. Then the results must be carefully considered and reflected on within the organisation, so that things can be changed to meet the customers' demands and expectations. Never conduct customer surveys and then allow them to gather dust in the corner of some office. That is a clearer statement to your people of what you think of your customers than anything you may ever say.

Involve all staff in maintaining the quality standard
All management must be committed to quality. And, at all costs, management must avoid expedient compromising of quality standards through urgent jobs and so on. By demonstrating this commitment, management must make all employees see quality as a key value of the organisation. One major way of achieving this staff commitment to quality is through the 'quality circle' concept. Quality circles are a means of involving employees in improving the productivity and quality of their own work. But the key to successfully instituting a quality circle programme is to create the appropriate attitudes and interests among the staff before instituting the programme. This must begin through unqualified commitment to quality standards by management. Some of the key steps in instituting a quality circle or similar type of programme are as follows:

1   Establish a steering committee.

2   Establish some broad objectives. Collect preliminary data to make before-and-after comparisons.

3   Define what the teams can and cannot discuss.

4   Advise personnel of the decision to implement the team concept. This is usually supported by a full educational programme on the nature of the standards that are being adopted, why the company is adopting the quality programme, how they may contribute, and any relevant background factors.

5   Train leaders in the skills of team quality improvement, which might include brainstorming, problem analysis, data gathering, setting priorities, presentation techniques, conducting team meetings, and then, once the leaders have been recruited, training the team members themselves.

6   The team collects data and analyses problems for it to deal with.

7   They then create solutions to those problems.

8   Solutions are presented to management.

9   Management decides the course of action and advises the teams, and the issue is dealt with from there.

Quality circles, and the other methods derived from and associated with them, will only be effective if they become part of the organisation's culture. The aim is to bring people to think and act in terms of quality. The teams, as such, are less important than the attitude, approach and skills that need to become embedded in the norms. Do this and do it well and your unit will flourish.

Keep a close eye on the cost of quality

Quality costs. Another problem for the production manager is the need to achieve the appropriate level of quality within definite cost constraints. There is a trade-off between the level of faulty output and the cost of eliminating all faulty output. Various statistical techniques are available that provide guidelines on the number of inspections necessary to achieve a given quality level. It is necessary to adopt a sensible approach to inspection operations. For instance, you should inspect after operations that are likely to produce faulty items, before costly operations, before operations that cover up defects, and before assembly operations that cannot be undone. And, on automatic machines, you should inspect first and last pieces of production runs, but perhaps not so many in between. And then you should inspect and test the finished product.

Adopt a trial-and-error approach to the cost of quality. Learn through trial and error the cost for your organisation of achieving certain quality standards. Learn about the relationship between cost input and achievable quality. The law of diminishing returns will be active here – that is, simply doubling the amount spent on quality control will not necessarily reduce rejects by half. At the same time, assess the steady improvement in market share that can be achieved through a product that is better value for money. See quality as one of your sales benefits.

Be personally committed to the quality standard

If you are not committed, do not expect your staff to be committed. This is a general rule of leadership. Your behaviour as well as your philosophy must demonstrate your commitment to quality. You are the leader. If you are unsure whether your behaviour exhibits these qualities, then ask an associate whom you trust. And listen carefully to the feedback. Learning about ourselves in this way can be threatening and sometimes painful. But unless someone tells us, we will never know. Learn to demonstrate commitment and not merely talk about it.

Ensure strong planning

Determining a manufacturing philosophy

Have a clear philosophy for the production unit

First you should consider the role of manufacturing in the overall organisational philosophy. For instance, is your organisation to be 'manufacturing driven' – that is, are you to produce a set of products first and then attempt to sell those products?

Too often the production manager's role is seen as a conservative one within the organisation. Some conservatism is essential; change in itself is not necessarily good. What has worked in the past is generally the safest yardstick for determining what we should do tomorrow. But the production manager should be open to change, conscious of both the technological advances within the industry and the need for the organisation to adapt to changing social structures.

The production manager needs to be aware of changing industrial relations, and changing social pressures affecting those industrial relations.

The production manager should also be aware of changes being pressed upon the organisation through its customers and the products its customers use. Products may need to be changed to bring them up to date with current customer needs. For instance, an item engineered using stainless steel may, under changing financial circumstances, be changed to mild steel, provided the customer can obtain it at a lower price. So producing the very best quality is not necessarily the philosophy to adopt; it is better to produce the level of quality that the customer needs.

What sort of role do you want to play in your organisation? Do you wish to be seen as proactive or reactive and conservative? To be the former, you need to think through your philosophy. What are you endeavouring to do with the production unit? How can you articulate that? And what tactics are appropriate to put that philosophy into practice, so that the production unit fulfils properly the role designed for it within the organisation as a whole.

Identify the production philosophy that provides a market edge

Should the sales department sell what the production unit can produce, or should the production unit make what the sales department can sell? For a mature, reasonable-sized manufacturing operation, it often takes more money to acquire a large, stable customer base than it does to put up a factory. Consequently, the production unit always needs to have a high level of consciousness of the customer and, in particular, changing customer needs. It cannot isolate itself to produce a product, leaving somebody else to sell that product.

What is the production philosophy that will provide your organisation with its market edge?

- Will your products be at the forefront of technological innovation? Or will they be slightly behind the state of the art, but of proven performance and reliability?

- Will you produce your products in a very high volume at highly competitive prices?

- Will your products be attuned to very specific customer needs? Or will your products be of a more general nature?

- Will your products be price sensitive so that low manufacturing costs allow a market advantage? Or will your products be highly reliable and specialised so that their cost becomes less important.

- Will your products be unique? Will you be able to come up with highly innovative solutions to new and old needs?

Answers to these questions will determine the nature of the production tactics you need to implement. For instance, if you are intending to offer products to the market that are price sensitive, and you are aiming to have the lowest production costs then clearly this is going to be very significant in terms of the tactics you will need to implement in your production unit.

While you should always be seeking effective cost reductions, this becomes crucial with such a philosophy. You need to think clearly about the production philosophy that provides your organisation with its market edge.

Determine your production philosophy

- What type of manufacturer are you, and what type of processes will you apply? For instance, are you producing products with technological processes that are well known? Are they products that could tolerate a high degree of design standardisation or component standardisation?

- Are you intending to operate at the leading technological edge? Are you likely to be technologically overtaken? That is, will technology be produced that could significantly if not radically alter the manufacturing costs in your industry? If so, what tactic can you put in place that will modify the impact of this? And how would you respond if it did happen?

- Is it essential for you to stay at the leading technological edge within your manufacturing operations? If, for instance, your market position is to produce high-quality products at very competitive prices, it is critical that you stay at the leading edge. Failure to do so will mean that you no longer have the lowest production costs, which could significantly undermine your market edge.

- How well do you understand your existing production processes? How well have they been researched? Is it possible for you to redesign and improve some of those processes'? When did you last carefully examine all your main production processes?

- How can you make choices between existing technology and new, innovative technology that may provide a market edge? And do you wish to undertake the necessary research and development?

Spend more time reflecting and working on these philosophical questions affecting your production unit. As a production manager, a critical aspect of your job is to think through the key conceptual issues facing your unit.

Integrate your production philosophy with the company's philosophy

- What is the company's existing brand image?

- Are you perceived in the marketplace as having up-to-the-minute innovative products? Or are you perceived as having steady, reliable products at sensible prices?

- Are you and your products perceived as being responsive to customer needs?

What has been the traditional pattern of manufacturing within the organisation? How do your staff see this pattern? What are their skills and attitudes? To start any serious revitalisation of the production philosophy of the organisation, you need to start with attitude. Time and effort need to be spent on ensuring that the production staff's attitude is in line with the philosophy you wish to implement.

Once you have thought through the production philosophy, particularly the key issues that need to be dealt with, then you should meet with your key production staff at a seminar or conference, and take them through the same philosophical issues that you have reflected on. In this way, you can begin to achieve some degree of philosophical consensus. Once they begin to see the concepts and the philosophy and the direction in which the organisation wishes to move, then it is possible to ask detailed questions about the tactical implementation of the philosophy, and to ask detailed questions about the current production processes and the nature of the products being produced.

Without reflecting on the philosophical questions of production processes and the position of manufacturing within the organisation as a whole, product and process reviews become arbitrary, one-off exercises lacking coherence and consistency. It is better that the whole organisation is taken along a particular path in an integrated, coherent way.

Develop a responsible attitude towards the customer

Too often the customer, and the demands and needs of the customer, are seen as intrusions into the otherwise orderly conduct of the business. Attitude is all. And this must begin with the attitude of the senior management.

- Are you responsive to customers?
- When did you last visit customers?
- How often do you visit customers?
- How often do you talk about customers with your senior staff?
- How often do you talk about customers with supervisors? Is every new idea that is considered within your production department assessed against the benefit that it will bring to your customers?

When you move around the production unit, watch out for attitudes inconsistent with rapid responsiveness to the customer and the customer's needs and demands. When such attitudes are countered, quietly but firmly correct them. Do so by asking people how they would feel if they were treated in such a way. Encourage interaction between your key departmental managers and supervisors and your customers. Involve all members of your production unit with your customers. Ensure that your key people, such as your dispatcher, know who to contact if there is some issue or problem to be resolved. Every month, come up with two new ideas about how the responsiveness and effectiveness of your production unit in serving the customer can be improved.

Capital investment

Understand that the true fixed cost is that of acquiring the market

For many large manufacturing operations, the plant required to manufacture the product to serve their customers may amount to perhaps £10-15 million. Acquiring the necessary customer base to absorb the product may easily require similar amounts of money spent annually on advertising.

Approach the problem from a different point of view. Imagine that the plant was burnt to the ground. Would the business be destroyed? Clearly you would have a major setback, but insurance and speedy reconstruction could see the business back in full operation with full sales levels within 18 months. Now imagine that the business lost its whole customer base. What then would happen to the business? Or take a less extreme version – let us say that the business lost 25 percent of its client base. What then? Clearly a loss of clients would be much more difficult to restore and to resolve than a loss of plant. A loss of clients – particularly if the loss took the business seriously below the break-even point – could, in fact, result in the winding up of the business. Clients are more important than bricks, mortar and plant. Serve them well.

Develop a matrix of suppliers integrated with existing plant

- Where are the bottlenecks in your plant?
- What outside suppliers do you have who could supply you the necessary services or components that would ease the bottleneck?
- What would be the impact of using those suppliers on your price and quality?

- How could you make those suppliers match the price you require at the necessary quality levels?
- Could you teach them?

Too often production managers see their production units as fixed entities with fixed capacity. This is an incomplete concept. A better concept is to see your plant in combination with all the suppliers and potential suppliers as a matrix of infinite capacity – or if not infinite, then certainly with a much larger capacity than that of your immediate plant.

In the first instance, identify every bottleneck in your plant, then ask the sort of questions above. Overcome every bottleneck by ensuring that an outside supplier meets the necessary components or service needs. This will inevitably shift the bottleneck. But then shift your focus, and find more suppliers to overcome the new bottleneck. Initially you might like to do all this on paper first, working through a thorough scheme whereby you can double the through-put of your plant – or at least increase the capacity of your plant to the level of the capacity of the highest-producing department or machine within it. In this way you will maximise the potential of your plant.

Regularly review all make-or-buy decisions

Should a component be made internally or purchased from an outside supplier? This question should be reviewed frequently for two main reasons.

First, assess the ability of a possible supplier to produce something more cheaply than you can change quite rapidly. The fact that they could not supply the product cheaply enough two years ago does not mean that they cannot do it today.

Second, within modern turbulent economies, new companies spring up very rapidly, often creatively employing technology that did not exist a few years before to produce components much more cheaply than the existing equipment and plant within your own organisation.

The decision whether to make or buy should be made on the following basis. First, establish what you could make the component for internally. Establish all the capital costs, and the operational costs, to obtain a net price for the component. The cost of making it should then be compared to the cost of purchasing it from the outside supplier.

Factors involved in assessing the supplier should be the likelihood of long-term availability, the ability of the supplier to meet the growth requirements of the organisation through a sensible period of time – say three to five years – and the ability of the supplier to hold their costs compared with the stability of your costs if you made the component internally. These factors should be discussed frankly with the supplier, who should provide full and open information. There is no place for secrecy at this time. The commitment should be long-term on both sides.

With this long-term commitment, business planning can be conducted effectively, the net result being better prices and a better supply situation for both parties. The make-or-buy decision should be taken very seriously whenever your own plant requires upgrading. The analysis of whether to invest in the new equipment or to buy the component from outside should be done using the full capital-expenditure assessment criteria normally used before purchasing brand-new plant. Do not treat it as merely an add-on to existing plant. Each time you should go back to basics and reassess the whole decision.

Adopt one system for assessing capital expenditure
Decisions concerning capital expenditure should consist of three primary elements.

- There should be some sort of problem analysis to assess the overall nature of the decision and whether or not it is in line with the corporate strategy as a whole.

- There should be a detailed financial analysis, consisting of either a net-present-value analysis or an analysis using a payback method.

- There must be an act of judgment.

Before doing a detailed capital assessment of a project, ask questions such as:

- Does this project fit within the overall strategic direction of the company?
- Will this project further enhance the company's strategic position within its chosen markets?
- What is the underlying reasoning behind this project?
- Is it consistent with the philosophy of the organisation?

If the answer to all these questions is yes, then the project may proceed to the next stage of analysis. Generally, this should be a potential-problem analysis examining the possible pitfalls of the project. Often many projects can be ruled out at this stage because of the problems associated with their implementation, despite their potential benefits.

The financial analysis will typically take one of two forms. First, the net-present-value technique discounts the value of the stream of after-tax cash-flows back to the present. The capital good with the least net present value is preferred if we want the one with the least cost, and the one with the greatest net present value is preferred if we want the one producing the greatest profits. The word 'net' suggests that all the cash flows are taken into account, both in-flows and out-flows.

The advantages of this system are that it considers the time value of money, discounting future returns and costs back to the present. It is commonly used in business. And it considers all the cash flows over the entire economic life of the capital good.

The disadvantages are that it requires complex compound-interest calculations. It is more difficult to explain and understand. And the selection of the discount rate is critical. Widely divergent rates can result in different investment decisions. It is at this point that company policy is critical. That is, the company must determine the discount rate it is to use and then stick by that discount rate, ensuring that all capital-expenditure proposals are measured using the same discount rate. Regardless of whether this discount rate adequately reflects current inflation levels and so on, it is consistency that is the key, because only then can apples, as they say, be compared with apples.

Finally, the net-present-value method can be inappropriate for comparing investments with unequal first costs.

The second method is the payback-period method. This method answers the question: How long will it take to get back our original investment less the salvage value through savings and operating expenses or other profit improvements for each capital good?

The assumptions that underlie this method are that investments that return the original investment faster are more profitable, that investments with fast paybacks are less risky, and that investments with fast paybacks allow the firm to reinvest its capital in new revenue-generating projects and thus relieve capital funds shortages.

The advantages of this system are that it is quick and easy to compute and requires no compound-interest calculations. It is easily explained and understood, universally used, and considered as a standard tool. It is most effective for firms with cash shortages and can be used for comparing investments with unequal first costs.

The disadvantages are that it does not consider returns after the payback period, it does not compound or discount future earnings of costs or consider the time value of money, and it builds in a short-range investment bias. It is also inappropriate for capital assets with net cash outflow. For example, a new machine performing a new operation may have cash outflows throughout its entire life, so a payback period cannot be calculated.

These factors are summarised on the following chart.

The advantages and disadvantages of the net-present-value method

Advantages	Disadvantages
1. Considers the time value of money; discounts future return and costs back to the present.	1. Requires complex compound interest calculations
2. Commonly used in business	2. More dificult to explain and understand
3. Considers all cash-flows over the entire economic life of a capital good.	3. The selection of a discount rate is critical; widely disparate rates can result in different investment decisions
	4. Can be inappropriate for comparing investments with unequal first costs.

The advantages and disadvantages of the payback-period method

Advantages	Disadvantages
1. Quick and easy to compute - requires no compound interest calculations	1. Does not consider returns after the payback period
2. Easily explained and understood	2. Does not compound or discount future earnings or costs; does not consider the time value of money
3. Universally used - considered a standard tool	3. Builds in a short-range investment bias
4. Most effective for firms with cash shortages	4. Inappropriate for capital assets with net cash outflows - for example, a new machine performing a new operation may have cash outflows throughout its entire life, so a payback period cannot be calculated
5. Adapts to comparisons of investments of unequal first costs	

Follow up all investment proposals

Seldom, if ever, are investment proposals followed up thoroughly to ensure that the project performs precisely as was predicted in the preliminary cash-flows and projections used to assess it in the first place. Reverse this. From today on, be sure that every proposal that is accepted and implemented is followed up through the duration of the planning period and the analysis period used to assess the proposal and so ensure that the project in fact performs as was originally intended. This is likely to be embarrassing in many instances. But it is extremely valuable information for the organisation.

Maintain a file of ideas for capital projects

All companies have more projects than money. Maintain a file of good project ideas that have been reasonably fully analysed, so that, if the opportunity should arise, they can be readily reinstated, re-analysed, and implemented when the cash is available. This file could consist of no more than an A4 ringbinder (or a computer file) with a two-page outline and analysis of each project. The file should be reviewed every budgeting period, and those projects that are regarded as still viable should remain in the file while others are discarded. Thus the file will remain a vital list of possible projects considered still relevant to the organisation.

Forecasting and planning

When forecasting sales, use historical data for projections

This is the first of two major sales-forecasting techniques. It uses historical data and extrapolates these data into the future. Various formal techniques can be applied to the data to provide a medium- to long-term trend. These may include linear regression, moving averages, exponential smoothing, and so on. Alternatively, sales can be plotted on graph paper to extrapolate the trend. These days there are various computer software systems available that will accept historical data, smooth it out, and extrapolate it into the future to give you a sales trend. All these techniques are very helpful. They're based on one fundamental fact: future sales trends will reflect historical sales trends. Using these techniques, if sales for the coming twelve months are to be higher than sales for the previous two or three years, then you need to have done something or be planning to do something extraordinarily different. In effect, historical sales trends reflect the word of mouth within your market. If you have a regular sales growth of 10 or 12 percent a year, you can regard your word of mouth as growing at that sort of rate. If you're suddenly seeking a 25 percent growth in any one year, you will need to do something extraordinary to increase the rate. You should bear in mind, of course, that the historical trend may reflect the growth in your industry rather than an increase in your market share. This makes it doubly important that you improve your word of mouth so that you do increase your market share. If you do not do something extraordinary and different from what you have done in the past, do not expect to get the extra increase.

Use the sales team to predict customer- by-customer sales
The second most significant technique for forecasting future sales is to ask customers. This is called the assignable-cause technique. Ask each sales representative to discuss with every client what they're going to use in the coming year. Then, simply by adding up all those predictions, you can end up with a sales forecast for the year. Alternatively, apply the judgment of the sales representatives and sales managers to the problem by getting them to identify every customer in their client base and to assess and judge how much each of them is going to take in the coming year.

We now have two forecasting techniques. One is based on the extrapolation of historical data and the other is based on the assignable cause. One can be regarded as top-down forecasting and the other as bottom-up forecasting. The effectiveness of your forecasting will not depend on which technique you use, for you should use both and then seek to analyse and reconcile any differences between them.

One technique for assessing sales projects involves examining the probability that the sales will be achieved. For instance, let us assume that a particular customer is projected to purchase 5,000 units of product and that the probability for achieving that is 70 percent as assessed by the salesperson. Then, within the forecast, you can multiply the 5,000 units by the 0.7 probability to come up with a figure of 3,500 units. That is what goes into the forecast. This reduces the forecast according to the likelihood of the sales coming through.

When assessing your sales forecasts, there are a number of other factors that you need to take into account. The first is the growth of the last three years compared with general economic growth.

What has been your growth compared to general growth and to your industry's growth? And why has that occurred? It usually pays to know why. What changes are likely to occur in the markets? What social trends are occurring? What are the projections of economic growth during the planning period? Secondly, you need to maximise the ownership of the sales goal by the sales team. That is, with respect to this particular factor, it pays to carry out bottom-up planning as opposed to top-down planning. It does not usually pay to impose on your salespeople the budget they're expected to achieve. It usually pays to have them involved in the planning and the establishment of those budget figures.

Review projections of your economic indicators over the planning period. What's going to happen to industry? Is it going to grow, stay about the same, or decline? Use historical results combined with economic trends to produce a statistical top-down forecast. Sales projections from the sales team can then be used to develop an assignable-cause forecast, customer by customer, preferably by asking the customers or a given percentage of them what they're going to need.

Finally, compare the sales team's forecast with the statistical one. If they differ, ask why. Why is there a variation and how is it going to be reconciled? Apply judgment to blend all the information into the required forecast. You now have your sales forecast projected through the coming planning period. It will have to be modified according to economic variations, which to some extent you've already brought to account. Then, if the likely competitor response is going to be very strong, be cautious. If the likely competitor response is going to be about the same as last year, proceed positively. Or, if you expect the likely competitor response to be weak and getting weaker, then move boldly.

At all times, remember that the growth trend reflects the momentum of your company in your market. If you're seeking growth significantly different from what you've experienced in the past, then you will have to do something distinctly different.

Always have at least three forecasts

The forecasts you require are:

1 Break-even
2 Expected
3 Targets

Break-even defines bottom-line survival. It is the minimum level that is absolutely essential if the company is going to survive through the coming planning period. You need to know these figures. They should not, however, be given to any other members of the team, and should only be disclosed and discussed in private among the senior management team.

The **expected results** are less private, but they show where you expect the company to be. Again, they are not usually discussed outside the senior management team.

The third level comprises the **targets** that are set for the sales team. They should be above the expected level of result and should be pitched so that the sales team needs to stretch for them, but they also need to be achievable. If the sales targets are set so high that they become unachievable, the sales team will stop striving for them and may settle back to a dangerously lower level of sales. Targets are essential. If your budgets are not sufficiently close to actual sales results, it simply means that you're not putting sufficient time into planning or applying adequate techniques to establishing your sales forecast. There is no right technique; you need to carry out top-down and bottom-up forecasting and then reconcile the differences. And, once that is done, take into account industry and economic activity, as well as competitor activity.

Understand the production manager's role in sales forecasting

Typically, it is not the production manager's responsibility to generate the sales forecast, but it is important to understand how this forecast should be arrived at. The role of the production manager should be to establish a strong relationship with the sales manager, obtain his or her agreement that accurate sales forecasts are essential, then provide whatever assistance is necessary to ensure that they occur.

We've discussed annual forecasting. This, however, needs to be broken down into weekly sales goals for each salesperson. These goals add up to the eventual achievement of the monthly sales targets, which in turn add up to the achievement of the annual sales budget. It pays to have a weekly planning review meeting with your sales management colleagues. Thus, week by week, the salespeople are focused on the sales they are going to achieve that week and you can be party to their planning, thus helping with your own operations planning.

Above all, the production manager should ensure that both top-down and bottom-up techniques are applied and then compared and that the final sales forecasts are drawn from a blend of the two. The more data that is put into the forecast, the more accurate the forecast is likely to be.

Allow for limited variations in your production plan

It is not possible to plan everything or forecast everything. Variations can and will occur. The goal should be to contain the degree of variation. This means that the bulk of the manufacturing operation can be planned, and variations become variations on the theme, as opposed to fundamental shifts. Operate on the premise that surprises invariably cost money. Establish operational lead times related to the longest lead time of any supplier. This could mean that the production plan for tomorrow is fixed at 10am today. Alternatively, it could mean that the production plan for August is fixed on 8 May. The flexibility of your operation will be determined by its nature and by your creativity and energy at managing it vigorously.

Whatever the deadline for finally establishing the production run, it must be clearly communicated to the sales team. Then behaviour consistent with that deadline must be insisted on. Before the deadline of 10am today for tomorrow, or 8 May for August production, there may be a period of a day or a week or a few hours during which the production plan may be modified to a generally agreed extent – say 10 percent. When planning in May for August, this is almost certainly essential. Thus variations, when it is time to produce the goods, become variations on the overall direction of the plan and not fundamental changes to the plan itself. This type of philosophy is essential for highly profitable production units.

Use simple planning and control systems wherever possible

Adopt a few simple rules, and ensure that your staff live by the rules. For instance:

• Ensure that only one person is responsible for the production plan.

• Ensure that a customer's planning staff are able to talk directly to your planning staff at the lowest possible level. Use on-line customer planning where possible – for instance, connect your computer directly to the computer of your customer.

• Have visual inventory-control systems.

• Have lines on the factory floor and ensure that work in progress is placed within particular areas and that everybody knows where those areas are.

• When a salesperson comes in with an urgent order, only his customers' orders should be adjusted and the customers told - someone else's urgent order should not be displaced.

Perhaps most important: use training to instill a forward-thinking attitude in the staff. Encourage them to think clearly and effectively about future problems, production planning, and how they can best serve the customer.

New products

Encourage your staff to suggest new products and improvements

Avoid, at all costs, the 'not-invented-here syndrome'. Creativity can spring from any source, and will constantly surprise you. Effective product creativity is not limited to head office or research and development staff. Adopt two fundamental approaches in improving existing products and creating ideas for new products: the top-down and bottom-up techniques. The bottom-up technique is carried out by productivity- and profit-improvement teams on the shop floor. This occurs when quality circle teams seek to improve productivity and the effectiveness of existing products within their sphere responsibility.

From time to time, the same teams will come up with ideas for new products. Often, springing from their analysis of how to improve some existing product, an idea will germinate for a completely new product. This process should be thoroughly encouraged. In addition, from head office, from the general management, from the senior team, and from the research and development department, there should be top-down product development, based on market research and analysis of customer needs, also incorporating social changes and the changing needs of the client base. The bottom-up approach to improvement tends to be a bit-by-bit process. The top-down approach tends to involve large-scale changes to the product range and structures as a whole.

From time to time, a good idea may come from a quality circle team and be taken aboard by the research and development department, resulting in a wholesale change in product range and its rationalisation. This process should be available to your organisation. Be sure that your staff appreciate creativity. Anyone can be creative; it often depends on being in the right place at the right time for a new idea to suddenly appear. All ideas, however, require refinement, research and planning to be implemented effectively. The ideas themselves are not the key, at the end of the day, to profitability. Profits are based on good ideas tightly implemented. 'Good ideas with discipline' – make that the catch-phrase of your organisation.

When planning a new product, test all aspects before proceeding

There are four key phases in launching a new product.

- **Phase one: get the concept right.** Accept the barest of bare product proposals, provided it intuitively feels right and people believe in it. Don't formalise the process by demanding reports or setting up committees. Ask lots of questions, but don't restrict creativity by stomping all over people. Encourage people to proceed, but don't give them a preliminary budget. Seek a broad idea of markets, pricing, costs and capital required in profits. But don't seek firm projections or definite answers – at least not yet. Talk to people, especially possible customers. Back hunches, best guesses and reasonable data. But don't pretend you can quantify the unknown. (If Henry Ford had done quantified research, he might have decided there was no market for motor vehicles)

- **Phase two: test and refine.** Build and test lots of prototypes, but don't lock in the design too early. Establish a sense of urgency, but don't rush to the market in order to be the first or to beat a competitor. Test prototypes on customers. Don't assume that head office people know what the customer wants. Identify the initial market niche for the product. But don't assume this is the only use. It is merely the market you can identify in which a return can be made on the initial investment. Build a task force round the product champion. But don't steal the good ideas from the people who thought of them. And never reject a good idea because of its source. Push hard with good, objective questions, but don't blunt enthusiasm.

- **Phase three: go or no go.** Establish the product design and a business plan to include a production plan, a distribution plan and a marketing plan. But don't confuse analysis and numbers with shrewd judgment. Involve the initiators in the decision process. Allow them to hear the arguments and reasoning. Don't make secret or aloof decisions. Delay if important questions need to be answered. But don't procrastinate.

120

- **Phase four: planning and co-ordination.** Go through every step in the plan with the people who must implement the plan. But don't leave it to someone else's initiative at the time. Establish the objectives for each team, guiding it to work out how to achieve them. But don't issue instructions from head office. Work to gain co-operation and commitment by involving people. Don't allow interdepartmental competition. Allow various levels to consult directly to solve problems. Don't reinforce formal communications through committees or chains of command. Plan carefully. Get the concept right. Don't lock in a budget too early. Once the idea is beginning to be moved through the organisation and to be accepted, you may begin to formalise the planning process. Don't rush; take your time. Then, at the implementation phase, plan, plan and plan some more. Brief people, educate them thoroughly, and make sure that they understand precisely the behaviour expected of them.

These are simple steps; the problem is implementing them thoroughly.

Ask plenty of questions
Your questions should include the following:

- Is there a strong, moderate or mild need for the new product?
- Is the new product compatible with existing sales, distribution and service methods?
- What new methodologies might be required?
- What impact, if any, will the new product have on current organisational structure?
- Does the new product seem compatible with the corporation's existing technology?
- If not, does it appear to be within state-of-the-art technology? If so, can it be introduced and utilised?
- What is the preliminary estimate of the cumulative profits versus time?
- How does this compare with other new products currently being evaluated in the business plan?

- Is the projected return on investment acceptable?
- What are the projected availability and life of the new product?
- How do these compare with the projected marketplace window and corporate guidelines for product life?
- How will the new product affect the company's position within the industry?
- What impact, if any, will the new product have on existing products?
- Is it compatible with existing components?
- What standardisation and rationalisation can be achieved?
- To what extent can the product range itself be rationalised by eliminating features encompassed by the new product?
- What would be the effect on pricing and inventories?
- If the new product supersedes existing products, what phase-in, phase-out policy will gain the best marketing momentum without significant inventory write-offs for the affected products?
- What would happen if the product were not developed or introduced into the company now or in the future?

Question thoroughly. Take your time. Reflect.

Be cautious about new product implementation

Do not undertake a new product or project that, were it to fail, could bankrupt the company.

This seems obvious enough. However, in one's enthusiasm for a new product, it is easy to overstate the potential returns and to significantly understate the potential risk. Every new product has the potential to fail. One in ten typically does. Be cautious of any product falling into the range of what is known as the 'zero/infinity dilemma'. For instance, there is a very small probability that a nuclear power plant will fail. But if one does fail, the result can be catastrophic. Zero or very small probability is combined with extremely severe consequences if the probability becomes a reality. Apply the same philosophy to your new products. There may be a very small probability of failure, but be very cautious of any product or project that, should it fail, even if failure is unlikely, could cause bankruptcy.

Even if they don't fail, but merely become difficult, the size and severity of the potential failure will force management to focus resources on this particular project at the expense of other parts of the business, resulting in a loss of business momentum. Avoid projects that could result in such distortions.

You should also be very cautious about all new products or processes involving technology new to the company. Do not underestimate the length of time it takes for people to learn new technology. Be aware of the skill base of your company. If the new product requires you to go beyond the skill base of your existing personnel, then be very realistic about the length of time and the real cost that will be incurred for your company to absorb and master the new processes and technology. It takes longer than you think. It is harder to manage than it appears.

A manager is not merely a manager; a good manager in your business and industry will not necessarily be effective with some other technology or process. This requires intellectual flexibility that simply may not be there. Be cautious about new products, new processes or new technology. The learning curve will be longer than you think and more difficult. Finally, be wary about any new product or project involving an increase in the managerial resources of the company – for example, one requiring the supervision of large numbers of extra staff. Supervisory and managerial capabilities are another key skill within your organisation. If the new product or process involves increasing your staff numbers from, say, 150 to 300, then be very cautious indeed about it. While it may only be a duplication of your existing plant, with no additional technology, new skills will be required. A 300-person company is a different type of company from one involving only 150 people. And there is a real tendency to minimise the degree of difference. Things can quickly get out of control – budgets cease to be met, time scales expand, and projects end up costing a lot more than was initially planned. Again, be very cautious. Move slowly.

Distribution and customer service

Train despatch staff in positive sales behaviour

The people likely to have the most frequent contact with customers are your despatch staff. At the very least, these people should have a sharp awareness of the needs and problems of the customers they serve. Their attitude should be to ensure that customers get the product when they require it. The despatch team and supervisor should have clear goals. These goals should relate to:

- minimising the number of complaints about unfinished or incomplete orders
- maximising the accuracy of the paperwork (packing slips, invoices or whatever is appropriate)
- raising the level of involvement with customers (e.g. advising them if an order cannot be completed and explaining why).

Other goals should be ensuring that the product goes out in good order, and, while despatch staff are not responsible for checking the quality of the finished product, keeping their eyes open for defects that may have occurred through handling after final assembly of the product. All of these goals have one objective – ensuring that the customer is satisfied and retained as a customer.

Encourage communication between your customers and despatch staff

One of the keys to an effective production operation is close contact between the customer and your own organisation. If a product cannot be delivered, the customer should be notified. If an order can be only partially filled, the customer should be notified. And, under any of these circumstances, customers should be advised as to precisely when the product will be available or, at the very least, when they will be advised of final delivery. This means that there must be systems within your organisation that provide the despatch team with the necessary information on production schedules, hold-ups, etc. Have a simple and practical system for establishing priorities in dealing with customer deliveries. Hold regular meetings to discuss orders and customer pressures, exchanging information between the salespeople and the despatch team on which customers may be able to wait a little longer and which need to be served now. This is particularly important if there happen to be any delays or restrictions in the availability of products. Be sure that the despatch office is staffed by people who will handle customer enquiries with due tact and diplomacy and, at the same time, will take sensible steps to endeavour to sell additional product to customers. Despatch staff should be trained in elementary sales techniques and, in particular, telephone communication techniques. Ensure that despatch is seen as one of the key areas of customer contact.

Balance distribution costs against service levels

Be constantly aware of ways and means of distributing your product more cheaply than you distribute it now. But do not do so at the expense of reducing customer service and satisfaction.

Ensure that you have clearly stated distribution and customer-service goals. These goals must involve issues such as service levels a customer can expect, the response time of technical support people, lead times from the placing of an order to delivery, policy on incomplete orders, and policy on damaged or inferior-quality goods. Such things sometimes appear obvious, but in taking them for granted essentials may be overlooked. Review today your distribution system, customer-service policy, and dispatch processes to ensure that customers are indeed getting the level of service that you believe they should. And, if in doubt, ask your customers what they think of your service.

Have a coherent maintenance plan

Maintenance management is concerned with ensuring that plant and equipment produces its product at the lowest unit cost consistent with the safety of the work force. Issues of maintenance management include staff (skilled maintenance workers), the storage of parts, specialised repair tools and machines, maintenance planning, contingency planning, minimising downtime, safety, and minimising the cost of repairs. Ideally, you should have a clear plan for preventative maintenance. The appropriate level is always difficult to establish clearly. Such maintenance is, of course, intended to minimise the effect of normal wear and tear on the equipment. It will not overcome those breakdowns resulting from, say, the breaking of a chain, or from poor use.

The level of preventative maintenance has to be balanced against the overall cost of maintenance. The aim is to have the minimum total maintenance costs – that is, to have the minimum level of preventative maintenance consistent with the minimum level of lost production time due to breakdown and maintenance time. There is clearly a conflict between these two; it is always possible to increase the level of preventative maintenance, but the cost may be prohibitive.

Some compromise is essential whereby preventative maintenance costs are contained, having been related to the level of breakdown and maintenance stoppages and the risk of serious breakdown. To establish the appropriate level of preventative maintenance, you should keep a record of the breakdowns that have occurred, the typical pattern of breakdowns, and the cost of a breakdown, including repair costs, idle time, re-works and rejects.

Then estimate the reduction in breakdowns if preventative maintenance were increased and the increase in maintenance if the preventative maintenance were reduced. This can be done by establishing the nature of the breakdowns and identifying the type of breakdown that would have been avoided through preventative maintenance. The data can be used to calculate the expected breakdown costs, preventative maintenance costs, and total maintenance costs for each preventative maintenance policy. For example, say 48 breakdowns have occurred on 24 machines in 2 years. Thus there are typically 2 breakdowns per machine per month. The actual distribution of breakdowns may have been:

quarter one – 4	quarter two – 8	quarter three – 6
quarter four – 10	quarter five – 2	quarter six – 8
quarter seven – 4	quarter eight – 6	

A breakdown might typically cost £1,500. Fifty percent of the breakdowns would have been avoided through preventative maintenance, which is currently conducted once every six months and costs £6,000 for all 24 machines. We can apply a formula to this data: the number of breakdowns per month equals breakdowns known, plus or minus the proportion likely to be corrected, multiplied by a fractional alteration in preventative maintenance policy. The percentage is positive if there is to be an increase in the maintenance period and negative if the maintenance period is to be decreased. Then we can analyse the policy of preventative maintenance every six months, four months, two months or one month.

The number of breakdowns, on that basis, would be as follows:

- every six months – 2 (this is the current situation)
- every four months – 1.67 (calculated from 2 (breakdowns known) minus (2 x 0.5 (the percentage likely to be corrected) x 2/6 (the fractional alteration in the maintenance policy)
- every two months – 1.33 (2 – (2 x 0.5 x 4/6))
- every one month – 1.17 (2 – (2 x 0.5 x 5/6)).

Taking the average number of breakdowns per month, you can then calculate the cost of breakdowns and the cost of preventative maintenance per month to give a total cost.

Total policy cost	Average breakdowns per month	Cost of breakdowns £	Cost of preventative maintenance per month £	Total cost £
1 month	1.17	1,755	6,000	7,755
2 months	1.34	2,010	3,000	5,010
4 months	1.67	2,505	1,500	4,005
6 months	2.00	3,000	1,000	4,000
8 months	2.33	3,495	750	4,245
10 months	2.67	4,000	600	4,600

This table shows that there is little estimated cost difference between a four-month and a six-month policy. The actual breakdowns will rise above the level of estimated breakdowns as the length of the maintenance period increases. This is because of the assumption that all those breakdowns capable of being corrected by preventative maintenance will be corrected. This is less true the longer the maintenance period. Because of this fact, the policy should be reduced to four months in the example above. Work harder in a practical way at balancing the cost of maintenance against the cost of breakdowns.

Develop clear policies for maintaining plant reliability

Key goals for improving plant reliability include:

- **Goal one: reduce the frequency of breakdowns.** This might involve policies of preventative maintenance, using well-trained operators, providing extra machines, under-utilising equipment, arranging early parts replacement, or over-designing reliability into the components of machines. Any or all of these policies, and any others that may be relevant to your particular operation, should be applied.

- **Goal two: reduce the severity of breakdowns.** Policies might include increasing crew size, keeping stocks of repair parts, and increasing the capacity of facilities. Utilise modular designs and easily replaceable parts. (This is now very common in the computer industry.)

- **Goal three: provide standby machines.** These policies have different financial implications, which should be analysed in detail for your particular operation. Your policy options should be assessed against the financial implications, and the best policy should be implemented – one that balances the cost of having no breakdowns against the breakdown risk and the cost of a breakdown occurring. Learn to manage this conflict.

Develop contingency plans to cope with emergencies

Ensure that all your staff and supervisors know basic plant problem-solving routines, and where to obtain skilled assistance if these are insufficient. This fundamental tactic should be thoroughly entrenched in the behaviour of your staff. And it should also be supported by clear instruction sheets, or posters, or any other form of public display that reinforces the necessary behaviour.

Beyond this, specialist maintenance staff should have fully developed contingency plans of the 'what-if' variety. The level of development of the contingency plan should depend on the probability and seriousness of the particular contingency. For instance, there may only be a very low probability that a particular contingency will occur, but if it did occur it could totally halt production. It may involve a particular machine or operation – one that is highly reliable and unlikely to go wrong – but, if it did, every other process in the plant would be restricted. There should be a fully developed contingency plan to cope with the failure of this particular unit or operation. You should ask yourself: 'What would we do if this particular operation broke down?' That sort of thinking should pervade your whole maintenance department.

Invest more time in forecasting

Sales forecasts are frequently inaccurate because insufficient time is devoted to generating them. Both 'top-down' and 'bottom-up' techniques need to be applied. The top-down technique is based on the analysis and projection of historical data – for example, taking the last three or four years' sales and projecting them forward to the coming twelve months. The sales projection should then be modified by several factors. First, you should take into account the level of economic activity. Is the economy going to expand or is it contracting? Will there be a boom or a recession? Second, you should take into account any known competitor activity. Are your competitors becoming more aggressive, or less aggressive? Depending on your assessment of the competitor activity, you may modify your historically projected sales forecast up or down. Finally, what additional sales activities are you planning? Will you increase the number of salespeople? Will you undertake that major advertising campaign you delayed last year? Will you undertake any special sales promotions? Your historical data should then be modified according to economic circumstances, the level of likely competitor activity, and any particular extra sales activities that are planned for your own organisation.

Offer leadership

Managing consistently

Ensure that all supervisors know the behaviour they must adopt to be successful

Work with all your department heads and supervisors to establish clearly the essence of their job. What must they do to be truly successful? What must they control? What must they achieve This will take more thought and careful reflection than you might think. For instance, consider a polishing supervisor with a polishing department of 20 people. What are the key success factors for that department? These might include achieving a certain polishing standard, careful handling of the product once polished, and meeting through-put targets. Clearly, at least two of these factors can come into conflict. For example, careful handling of the finished product may conflict with the need to move it quickly through the department. Your department heads and supervisors should understand the key factors that need to be controlled in order for them to be successful in their jobs. Then they should determine how improvements can be implemented and what tactics should be applied. By creating clear images in the minds of your department heads and supervisors, you can make it clear to them how they need to behave and what they need to do in order to be successful. Then when you walk around you know what you are looking for.

Constantly stress the key production values

You clearly cannot do this unless you know what they are. And you derive these values in part from the philosophy that you are implementing within your production unit. Meet with your department heads and supervisors with a view to establishing, from within the team as a whole, the key values that will be implemented. Obviously, points of tension must be overcome. For instance, any conflict between the quality of the product and the need for good productivity needs to be identified, and creative solutions need to be adopted by all concerned.

If your product and brand image involve innovation and technical excellence, then clearly these values must be encompassed by the people within the heart of the organisation. Your staff must live and think technical excellence and innovation. These values must pervade their behaviour so that they act appropriately in all situations. If, on the other hand, you are aiming for a high degree of specialisation and standardisation, utilising technology that is well established and creating products that are price sensitive, with low manufacturing costs giving a market advantage, then that is how your people need to think. This becomes a key aspect of your philosophy from which essential values are derived. Your people need to review this and work out the details. Once the values have been established, ensure that you apply them yourself and reinforce them throughout the organisation.

Do not act in ways inconsistent with the key values

For example, if quality is your essential key value, never act in a way that is inconsistent with that value. If you want to push a very large job through your organisation or through your production unit and the job has been marginally costed, do not ask your people to adopt lower quality standards. Establish your values. Establish the behaviour and tactics consistent with those values. Then keep to them.

Check that your philosophy is being implemented

Stay involved. Praise, reprimand and set goals.

Be aware of what is going on. Establishing the direction for an organisation is not just a conceptual act; everybody in the organisation must live out the concepts day by day, with every decision they make.

As the person who has been most concerned with developing the philosophy, you need to be highly visible and highly involved in order to ensure that all of the multitude of decisions that are made within your organisation are consistent with that philosophy. When that is not happening, you need to act quickly. This can be done through a meeting, seminar, conference or training session. If you run a large production unit, you will almost certainly organise some sort of seminar or conference, in which all the key players get together and thrash out the values and tactics that are necessary. Then the managers and supervisors must go back and do the same thing within their own departments to ensure that all decisions are shaped by the philosophy that you want the organisation to pursue.

Ensure that the key disciplines of your business are followed

Every business and every industry has disciplines that are necessary for it to survive. These disciplines are part of the business. They are independent of the people. That is, a business in a given industry has key disciplines that must be followed if the business is to be profitable. The leadership problem is then ensuring that people's behaviour is consistent with those disciplines. For you to carry out this leadership role effectively, you must understand clearly the key disciplines in your production unit. Relevant areas might include waste control, service, delivery, innovation, quality, productivity and the implementation of known technologies. Whatever the issues and whatever the disciplines, you must enforce them in your business. If you do not do this, your business will be less effective than it would be otherwise.

Building a strong team of supervisors

Understand that people relate best to their immediate supervisor

Ensure that your supervisors supervise. They need to get to know their people. They need to understand what each of their team members has to do. They need to be able to get that across clearly to those team members. They need to be able to praise and discipline. They need to understand the importance of forging their staff into a team. The supervisors are the essential implementers within the production unit. They need to be effective, and to be supported vigorously, for they control the majority of the staff.

Ensure that supervisors understand they are the essential link between management policy and its implementation

Supervisors are essential. The effectiveness of your production unit can be largely determined by the effectiveness of your supervisory line of management. Raise the status of supervisors so that they see themselves as the link between management policy and the implementation of that policy. These are the people who know the details of your processes and operations. These are the people you need to talk to if you seek bottom-up productivity, expense control, and general performance improvement. These are the people who must be involved effectively if any changes are to be made. If you control your supervisory line effectively, you have control of the organisation as a whole. Success is having clear, direct, effective policy tightly and thoroughly implemented. In short, it is good senior leadership and strong supervision.

Develop a strong team spirit among supervisors

Supervisors can be left in a no-man's land, neither employee nor management. You need to be acutely aware of this potential problem. A strong team spirit should be developed among the supervisors. They need to understand their importance as the key implementers of management policy. And they need to be given status. Often conflict will occur between departments and between supervisors in different departments. This conflict should be converted to a competitive edge that spurs such department on to better things. It must never be allowed to degenerate into internal political strife, which disrupts the overall functioning of the organisation.

Walk around and observe and talk to your supervisors. Note what they are doing and note what they tell you. In particular, note the typical sorts of problems they bring to your attention. Then work on having those problems resolved. Do not ignore what they tell you. They know the reality of the day-to-day detail. It is this detail that you must control and manage in the direction you seek in order to realise your vision for the production unit. Every month, do at least one thing to enhance and consolidate the cohesiveness and effectiveness of your supervisory line. Such things might include social functions, training sessions, productivity reviews, visits, or the feedback of additional data on a monthly or weekly basis – whatever it takes. Strengthen your supervisory line, then use the increased control that you will be able to exercise and the increased leadership you will have in order to ensure the realisation of your vision.

Focus supervisors on the daily details

The supervisors are the doers. They get things done. Most of their time is consumed by the immediate pressures of the job. They do not and should not have large amounts of reflective time. They are the practical implementers. You should involve them in discussions on those practical details, exploring ways of improving those practical details, identifying the problems that they typically encounter on a daily basis, and then going away with this detailed information, reflecting on it, selecting from it the problems that are to be resolved during the next month, and then doing something about those. Keep your supervisors focused on the daily reality. But relate to them sufficiently, sufficiently often, and with sufficient intensity for them to feel that they are listened to and that they are involved and that management takes heed of what they say.

Ask questions to stimulate thinking

Ask questions about the detail of what staff do. How do they do it? Why do they do this or that? What is the purpose of a particular move? And so on. When gaining this information, deflect staff away from complaining and get them to focus on practical things that they can control and that can be implemented immediately. There will always be a temptation for them to tell senior management how the whole organisation should be run. Typically, this advice lacks perspective and the overview of senior management. Be patient but divert their creative effort into more practical things that can be influenced immediately by the supervisory line. Recognise that supervisors will not always have a broad enough perspective but it is important not to ignore their ideas and thus cause them to retreat and not contribute at all. The key is to focus their creativity so that their proposals can in fact be practically implemented. Satisfaction comes from identifying the problems you can overcome and overcoming them. Encourage your supervisors to live by this simple philosophy.

Do not destroy the team spirit of your supervisors

If you wish to destroy the team spirit of your supervisors, do the following simple things:

- Do not listen to them.
- Always tell them what they should do.
- Ignore the problems and issues that they bring to you.
- Never seek to motivate them (on the basis that they're supervisors and don't need to be motivated).
- Never consult them.
- Never get them together as a team.
- Encourage conflict rather than co-operation between the various departments and supervisors.

If you ever catch yourself adopting any of these habits, you should pause and reconsider.

Improve plant morale

Ensure that all supervisors know and work with their team

People relate best to their immediate supervisor. Encourage your supervisors to get to know their staff well – to know something about their families, their aspirations, their strengths and their weaknesses and to blend them into a team. Encourage your supervisors to have a daily round where every morning they say hello to all their staff. They should spend some time with each staff member at least once a week – that is, one day, in their daily round, they might say hello to four or five people but spend some time with the sixth, and the next day they might have a discussion with a different team member. It is important to make people feel that they are listened to and that they are key members of the company. It is only their immediate supervisor who can achieve this. However, you, as production manager, or the manager above the immediate supervisor, can have an important effect. For instance, if a staff member has done particularly well at some task or has achieved some goal, then the supervisor should let the manager know so that the manager can come out and say, 'Well done, this is great'. That's beginning to use authority and leadership within the plant in an appropriate way to keep morale high.

Know staff names and personal details

If you run a large production unit of several thousand people, it is difficult to know all their names. But careful planning can circumvent some problems.

A managing director of a supermarket chain frequently toured the branches. There were 5,000 staff. It was impossible for him to know the names of every staff member. But before visiting a branch, he would get the staff list. He would make notes about any exceptional people or unusual circumstances or personal problems. He would be sure to have thoroughly memorised the names of all supervisors within the branch and many of the other staff. So when he went into the branch he could call people by name and mention some personal detail about them. You should apply this principle yourself.

Involve production staff in resolving customer problems

As part of striving for improved customer awareness among your production staff, you should involve them in resolving complaints and problems that arise from customers. This can be achieved in various ways: arranging weekly meetings where customer issues are raised, attending sales meetings, and making particular production supervisors responsible for resolving problems concerning specific customers who are under the control of one of the sales supervisors. The ways and means of achieving this focus are many and varied. Select two and do them. The most critical thing is for you, as production manager, to have a positive attitude towards these issues and towards your relationship with the sales manager. There will always be a tension between sales and production. However, the tension and natural politics that exist between the two divisions should not get in the way of the fair, sensible and objective resolution of problems and complaints that arise from customers.

Ensure that production staff know key customer staff

The 'just-in-time' philosophy depends greatly on problems being dealt with at an appropriate level. For instance, your key production supervisor should know, or at least know how to contact, the key supervisor on the client's staff. That way any issues, questions, queries, problems, delays and alterations can be dealt with quickly, efficiently and – hopefully – just in time. The setting up and carrying out of this just-in-time philosophy takes careful planning and a great deal of attention to the relationships that exist between production staff and members of the client's staff. Setting up these relationships, and ensuring that your key production supervisors know who to contact, is the responsibility of the production manager.

Advise your staff of successes

There are two types of success that your staff should be informed of. The first is the overall success of the company or the unit production department. The second is much more direct and personal: the success that they have achieved in the last two days, week, month, or whatever time period is appropriate. Production staff should receive a weekly report outlining the success that they have had during that week. The report should relate specifically to their behaviour – that is, the number of units produced, the number of machines set up, the number of finished articles despatched, or whatever is an appropriate measurement. And individuals should be able to relate the measurement directly to their own behaviour. On an even more immediate level, get into the habit establishing 'one-minute goals' with production staff. If you are walking through the plant and you see a particular task that needs to be done, or you wish to delegate something, then offer it to the individual as a goal, backing this up with an agreed time when you will check, or when the individual will inform you that the goal has been achieved. The critical thing when setting up these goals, is to be sure to check that they have been carried out. If staff are not performing, offer them their weekly information without comment, but staff who are performing should be praised and encouraged publicly. In this way, encourage staff to strive for success and to enjoy receiving weekly feedback on that success.

Create celebrations involving all staff

A productive culture or climate within your production unit will blend discipline, performance pressure, and inspiration. Avoid motivation based on large amounts of emotional energy – the 'ra, ra, ra' style of motivation. Rather, base motivation on clear, firmly set goals. Then bring about a quiet resolve to realise those goals. Seek motivation based on calmness and determination.

Balance this quiet resolve with energetic social releases and celebrations, for whatever reason – the opening of a new plant, somebody's birthday, or the fact that it is the week before Christmas or the week before the summer vacation. Create a reason to get everybody together to celebrate and enjoy themselves and mix in a social situation. This is most important for the establishment of team spirit. One way to develop team spirit is to form a social club. Ideally, the social club should be the idea of the staff themselves. They might seek to join the local business football or tennis league or to hold regular social functions of some sort. The social club should be supported by the company, and facilitated by the company, but not necessarily be seen to be the vehicle of the company. Work harder to blend the necessary discipline with social release and inspiration to achieve better motivation in your plant.

Train frequently

There are three fundamental types of training and they should not be confused.

• The first is training specific to the company. This may be about jobs, product or administrative systems, or it may be an induction course.

• The second is general training related to the job – for instance, keyboard skills for computing, engineering skills on a lathe or a router or some other large machine, or mechanical skills for dealing with motor vehicles, or for other forms of plant maintenance.

• The third is developmental training for improving leadership skills.

A blend of training, balancing these three types, is essential, but they must not be confused. Be sure to plan for a balanced framework of training with your department. That is, be sure that everyone has the appropriate knowledge that is unique to the company – knowledge of products, systems, administration, responsibilities and so on. In addition to that, provide for the necessary skills that the company needs but that are not necessarily unique the company, such as engineering and computing skills. Finally provide for the application of these skills through the effort of others. That is, provide for the necessary leadership, supervisory and management skills. This requires a different sort of training again. In addition to all of this formal training, there should be a comprehensive and focused approach to on-the-job training. There should be regular, small meetings, focusing on improving this process or that procedure or the quality of a product or efficiency of a job or the speed of a machine.

You should seek to create a climate within your organisation in which supervisors, managers and operators are always striving to improve and raise the performance level of all staff. Where one particular operator or supervisor can do particularly well, ask that individual to train others in order to raise the overall standard. In other words, use your own staff to train other staff in the tasks they are good at.

Training is the most effective way to improve performance. Attitudinal training is essential. If the attitude is right, the skills will be applied and deficiencies in skills will be overcome.

Set an example by doing your job well

If someone was to do your job extremely well, what are the two or three or four things that they would control? What are the key success factors in your job? A sports team sets out to win. But that is not enough; it requires tactics – those elements that will guide its behaviour on the field of play. For instance, a football team, while striving to win, may determine to do so by playing it very tight, not making long passes, and driving constantly through the other team's defensive line. Thus the factors of keeping it tight and driving through the opponents' line become the tactics guiding immediate behaviour on the field. They are the tactics that lead to the overall goal of winning.

Your task is to make a profit, or at least to contribute to the profitability of your company. What are the tactics you propose to adopt to do so? Where are the opportunities? Will you focus on better through-put? Improved customer service? Reduced waste? Better control of operational overheads? What are the opportunities? What are your tactics? Doing your job well requires you to think very carefully. Then, from your thinking, come the guiding tactics to focus the efforts of your people. You must lead and cajole and inspire and discipline them to act in such a way that those tactics are realised and implemented effectively. You must decide the direction, involve and focus the people, enthuse them, keep a close eye on the detail, follow up to make sure that success is achieved, and measure that success. To lead from the front is not to do the job of the others but to do your own job well and be seen to do it well.

Encourage your supervisors to lead as you do

You set the tone in your team. To illustrate, imagine that you interacted with one of your staff in such a way as to cause them a small slight. You were busy, or worried about your family, or worried about a report to your boss, and because of this, you spoke a little more abruptly and harshly than you might otherwise. The offence is no major issue. You perhaps did not even notice. But this offence is going to take (say) 36 hours to work out of the system of your staff member. Now let's assume that 20 hours later you do a very similar

141

thing. Again, it is a small event below the level of your consciousness. You didn't even notice. Now slight builds on slight; it's going to take perhaps 45 to 50 hours to work out of their system. And let's say, 20 hours later, the same type of thing happens. We now have a situation where your relationship with this individual is deteriorating, bit by bit. And while it may recover for some time, if this is the general nature of your interaction then the climate in your team will slowly worsen.

This is the precise nature of the leadership I am referring to. Management of the climate in your team is not something you do twice a week or three times a year; it is a consequence of every interaction between you and your team members.

To manage the climate is to manage the detail of your behaviour on an ongoing basis. The second form of leadership of which you must be aware is directional leadership. This is where you create the direction to focus your team's efforts. This is perhaps an occasional act, in that once the direction has been set it usually lasts for some period – a few days, a few weeks, a few months, or even a few years. But once the direction is set, it is the first sort of leadership, the interpersonal leadership of your team, that will determine the success of your plan.

Become more aware of your behaviour towards your supervisors. Be firm but fair, supportive but disciplined. Once you are getting it right, encourage your supervisors to lead their people as you lead them. In that way the climate will slowly improve through the whole of your organisation.

Set clear goals

It is essential that people know exactly what is expected of them. They should have a clear definition of responsibility. Regular tasks and their priorities must be clear and well understood.

When leading your team, apply the following rules:

1   Be sure that they know precisely what is expected of them – from general overall direction to daily tasks, immediate priorities, and any one-minute goals that you may give them in response to specific problems.

2   Once they know what is expected of them, be sure that they have the necessary skills. That is, train them in the specific company, product or administrative area, as well as specialised skills such as engineering or computing, and also ensure that they have the necessary behavioural, leadership and supervisory skills.

3   Once they have achieved rules 1 and 2, expect them to get on with it. At the same time, expect them to come to you if any unusual problems or issues arise, without encouraging them to ask you to solve their problems.

Make it clear to people what is expected of them, be sure they know how to do it and that they can do it, then expect them to get on with it.

Involve staff in improving processes, products and operations

The table that follows lists those things that satisfy people in their jobs and build morale ('satisfiers') and those things that merely maintain their behaviour and do not encourage them to make any emotional commitment to what they are doing ('maintainers'). Concentrate your efforts on those things that give satisfaction. Seek to involve people in what they are doing. Operate as a team. Ask them how things can be improved. Then give recognition and rewards to those who contribute successfully. Your people are your greatest resource. Put more effort into effectively involving them in their jobs and in the achievement of the company's goals.

Maintainers	Satisfiers
Salary	Achievement
Job security	Earned recognition
Job status	The work itself
Company policy and	Increased responsibility
administration	Advancement
Working conditions	Growth
Fringe benefits	
Manager's competence	

Make supervisors supervise

The job of a supervisor is to organise the work on the factory floor, or in the office, so that the people who are doing the work can concentrate their efforts on what they have to do.

Do not set supervisors apart from the people they must supervise. Avoid involving them in long management meetings where much of what is discussed is not relevant to them. When first seeking to involve them in improving quality, processes, products or operations, be aware that they are likely to be sceptical and, at first, cynical. Be patient and persist. Encourage them to put forward ideas, and be sure to implement some of those ideas.

When managing by walking around, ask about how they have got their people organised. Enquire about the work flow. Your supervisors should be aiming to have a steady flow of work coming to the operators – enough to keep the operators busy without having to stop to look for more work, but not so much that work which has backed up behind them demotivates them. Show your supervisors how to achieve this balance.

Be sure that all staff know who they report to

Have a clear chain of command. Generally this works best. Be sure that the chain of command is as short as practicable. You want a flat organisation. Seek to retain a supervisor-to-employee ratio of 1 to 8 or thereabouts. It should be less if a supervisor is managing operators with widely divergent tasks. It could be a lot more if a supervisor is managing people with very similar tasks. Then organise the plant into sensible and consistent departments or units, with a supervisor controlling the operations within each. The system should be simple, practical and as flat as possible, with everybody understanding clearly what is expected of them.

Never compromise on key standards and values

The appropriate quality is essential. Do not compromise quality for expediency. Shared values are also critical. They might include the importance of the customer, ongoing involvement of staff in quality improvement and the improvement of processes and products, regular information about the performance of the company, a vigorous response to problems, seeing problems as opportunities, sharing and enjoying one another's company and coming to terms with one another socially as well as professionally, taking pride in one's work and craftsmanship, and the desire to succeed and be successful – whatever the values are, respect them. If you are unclear about the values, then perhaps you should hold a workshop to discuss and agree on them. Such values are not things that you can force your people to adopt; they must arise from within the heart of your people. They must be owned, and once owned they must be respected.

Retain simple production systems

Keep it simple. For instance:

* Have a visible production board.
* Ensure that all key staff knows how it works.
* Have only one person responsible for production priorities.
* Have only one person responsible for changes to the production schedule.

When a salesperson comes in, or when the sales manager comes in with an urgent job, ask which job he or she would like to put to the bottom of the list so that the new one can go in.

Conduct your forward planning with precision and care. Adopt some rules that determine when the production plan cannot be changed. For example, the production plan may be changed up to four weeks prior to production being scheduled. Inside four weeks it may only be varied by plus or minus 10 percent. Then, with one week to go, no changes may be made to the production plan. There is a natural tension between the necessity of production scheduling and the determination of the sales team to meet every possible customer demand. This has to be understood and successfully negotiated. One way is to adopt a 'just-in-time' philosophy so that the supervisors within your factory know and have contact with the supervisors and the clients. This enables key people to discuss problems and issues and do something about them before they become major tensions between the client and supplier. The production board may simply be a chart on the wall of the production office, or it may be a spreadsheet in the computer. Either way, the simple rules above still apply. The essential quality of these rules is that they are to be lived, not merely discussed. Your job as production manager is to identify such simple rules and encourage your unit to live by them.

Hold short, effective production meetings

Keep all meetings short and to the point. Be sure that you have a clear agenda that you know exactly what you want to get across, and stick to the agenda. But, in keeping to the agenda, be sure that you listen and appreciate what is being said to you by your people. Keeping to the agenda should not be an excuse for you to overpower their views. Ensure that all your key staff are advised of plans and changes to plans. One of the most familiar cries in many production units is 'Nobody tells us anything'. Hold enough meetings to keep key staff properly informed.

Have a round of regular meetings. They do not necessarily need to be frequent. The duration between meetings may vary depending on the urgency of the issues being considered. Become used to adopting this flexible approach. But be sure that there is an adequate information flow system to ensure that people are kept informed and feel involved even if there is a month between meetings. This can be achieved via notice boards, regular memos, or simply having an informal word-of-mouth system where information is fed through people without necessarily having formal meetings.

Develop the habit of holding short meetings on the factory floor. If you have a particular problem or issue to be considered, and it is necessarily going to involve four or five key supervisors, quickly go down, walk around them, agree a time when it is suitable to meet, tell them what the topic is, tell them you'd like them to think about it a little bit in the meantime, then hold the meeting. The meeting does not even necessarily have to be held sitting down. It might only take 15 to 20 minutes, for which you can stand, discuss the topic, agree what has to be done, then return to the task. Avoid using meetings as an excuse to get together and talk. Do that in your inspirational times, either socially, after work, or during lunch hours. By conducting yourself in this way, you constantly give urgency to your team. The urgency comes about through your actions, but be sure that your personal conduct at such meetings is not frenetic. Act in a calm, deliberate and precise manner, but in a manner that gets things done quickly and effectively.

Avoid demotivating people

Build a climate of co-operation by being co-operative. But being co-operative does not mean unnecessarily giving way to people's demands. Have a clear set of values and simple philosophies that you expect people to live by. Stress constantly the attitude that the unit succeeds if everyone does their bit, and that everyone has an important part to play. Use this concept to increase the stature of every employee in the eyes of every other employee. Stress that the individual sweeping the factory floor is as important as anyone else in the plant.

Be sure to get to know your key people as people. Socialise with them. Learn something about their families and their interests. And recognise their successes in their life beyond the plant.

But, at the end, it is easier to demotivate people than to motivate them. All you need to do to really demotivate your people is:

- Be sarcastic.
- Never encourage people.
- Seek out opportunities to make them feel small.
- Ignore constructive criticism, suggestions and honest questions.
- Run a one-man show and never allow your people to influence you.
- If they make an impression on you, don't let them know it.
- Be indecisive and weak.
- Never communicate.
- Play favourites.
- Have special friends and enemies.
- Take it out on those you dislike.
- Accept all credit when things go right. Blame other people when things go wrong.

- Be obviously unethical.
- Be a boaster; always talk about 'I, me and mine'.

You can motivate people in one of two ways.

First, you can do things that will influence them sufficiently to increase their commitment and the amount of energy that they contribute.

Second, you can stop doing those things that tend to demotivate people. Re-examine the list above. If any of those things from time to time appear in your behaviour, then eliminate them and improve the motivation of your people

INDEX